STREAMING TV SHOW

The Complete Guide to Launching your own TV Show

Dee Daniels

ABOUT THE AUTHOR

My name is Dee Daniels. I'm a journalist, broadcast professional, and technology startup serial entrepreneur from Chicago. I began my career as a reporter for the *Chicago Tribune* and later launched a women's news partnership with the *Chicago Sun Times* through my own publication, **Noir Women**, which led to interviews with notable figures like Michelle Obama and Delores Jordan (Michael Jordan's mother).

My broadcast journey has included on-air and producer roles at WEJM and WNUA FM radio in Chicago, as well as co-production work with E! Entertainment Network. After spending a decade as a senior executive producer at World Talk Radio Network—focusing on live-streamed and on-demand content—I founded **World Broadcast Network T** and the **Women's Broadcast Network**, delivering live-streamed programming on Apple TV, Roku TV, Amazon Fire TV, and Android TV.

As an early adopter in technology, I've launched several ventures aimed at empowering women and girls in media and tech. These include **Digital Diva 2.0**, championing coding and digital broadcasting opportunities, and **Bitcoin Clutch**, a peer-to-peer platform supporting women entrepreneurs and nonprofits. I'm also a proud mom and grandmother who splits her time between Chicago, Phoenix, and Los Angeles.

TABLE OF CONTENTS

CHAPTER 1

The Rise of Streaming TV

Streaming television has rapidly transformed how people watch and share content across the globe. What began as a niche concept, often limited by slow internet speeds and smaller audiences, has evolved into an industry that challenges traditional broadcasting in every entertainment corner. Viewers now have the freedom to choose what to watch and when to watch it, creating a personalized experience once unimaginable in the era of scheduled programming. This shift speaks to a cultural change, where flexibility and viewer engagement take center stage, and technology continues bridging gaps that previously limited access.

The relationship between the host and the audience is at the heart of this transformation. Instead of passively tuning in at a designated time, viewers tune in on their own terms, anywhere in the world. This dynamic opens up endless possibilities for new voices and established personalities to reinvent themselves. It's a democratization of content that has empowered creators to reach audiences without the constraints of network approval or rigid broadcast schedules. In short, streaming has redefined what it means to produce and consume entertainment, laying the groundwork for a revolution that continues to unfold daily.

A Brief History of Broadcasting

Broadcasting began with the simple magic of radio, where families would gather around a single device to listen to live shows, news bulletins, and musical performances. In the early 20th century, radio served as the primary method of mass communication, enabling information to travel quickly across vast distances. The experience was communal, drawing people together to share in the excitement of news stories or the drama of fictional programs. This foundation laid the groundwork for what would become one of modern history's most influential communication mediums.

Television emerged a few decades later, changing the landscape by adding visual elements that captured the imagination of viewers worldwide. Early television sets were bulky, and the picture quality was limited to black and white. Despite these limitations, the novelty was irresistible, and families adapted their routines around specific broadcast times. As television technology advanced, color broadcasts introduced a new layer of excitement. The ability to see events and scripted shows in full color turned TV into an even more immersive experience, further solidifying its place in daily life.

By the time color TV became widespread, major networks dominated the airwaves. Viewers planned their evenings around signature programs, waiting patiently through commercial breaks for their favorite shows to resume. This "prime time" model gave rise to landmark moments in television history, from groundbreaking sitcoms to unforgettable live events. Cable services joined the scene, offering specialized channels that catered to more diverse interests. Sports, music, documentaries, and movies each found dedicated spaces on the channel dial, reflecting the evolving demands of a growing television audience. Yet, even with more channels available, there were still fixed timeslots and schedules that viewers had to follow.

The game changer arrived when the internet became accessible to a broad audience. Early online video platforms struggled with dial-up connections, making the streaming experience choppy and frustrating. Despite these hurdles, media pioneers saw the potential for something unprecedented: viewers could choose what to watch and when to watch it, breaking free from the rigidity of broadcast schedules. As technology improved and high-speed broadband became commonplace, streaming platforms could host entire content libraries on demand. This paved the way for companies like Netflix to shift from mailing DVDs to offering instant online access to thousands of shows and movies.

The ease and convenience of on-demand viewing revolutionized how people consumed entertainment. Audiences became more selective, picking programs that matched their unique tastes and personal schedules. By watching shows through computers, smartphones, or smart TVs, viewers no longer had to rush home to catch a program at a set time. This freedom encouraged a binge-watching culture, where entire seasons could be consumed in a single weekend. It also propelled a wave of original content creation as streaming services invested heavily in exclusive series and films to attract subscribers.

Today, the lines between traditional broadcasting and online platforms continue to blur. Live events, sports, and even major network television programs are often simulcast or offered on streaming services, giving viewers a choice they never had before. The internet's global reach means that people can watch the same show regardless of where they live, and up-and-coming creators can bypass legacy networks to connect with audiences directly. This open environment has fundamentally changed the flow of entertainment and how people interact with it, marking a monumental shift in the history of broadcasting.

Why Streaming Has Taken Over

Streaming services have experienced remarkable growth thanks to technological breakthroughs, evolving viewer expectations, and shifts in the broader entertainment landscape. High-speed internet connections have become increasingly accessible, allowing users across the globe to load high-definition video in seconds. As networks improved, so did the devices people used. Smartphones, smart TVs, and tablets are now commonplace, making it easier than ever to watch shows and movies while on the go or from the comfort of home. This seamless accessibility has changed how audiences approach entertainment since streaming no longer relies on cumbersome hardware setups or rigid timetables. Viewers can tap an app and dive into their favorite series whenever it suits them.

Another key factor is the rise of original programming on streaming platforms. Companies recognized early on that having exclusive, high-quality content could set them apart in a competitive market. This pushed services to invest heavily in producing new shows and films, drawing audience's eager for something fresh. Word-of-mouth recommendations and social media chatter then propelled these programs to global recognition, further strengthening the position of streaming as a primary source of entertainment. Viewers started to see that some of the most talked-about series were being made exclusively for streaming services, making traditional TV feel behind the times. The freedom to experiment with different genres and storytelling approaches also attracted creative talents who wanted more control over their work, raising the bar for quality across the board.

Consumer habits have changed dramatically in recent years due to busy lifestyles and an increasing desire for convenience. People no longer want to schedule their evenings around a TV guide. The flexibility of streaming lets them tune in when they're available, reducing the need to plan around fixed broadcasting hours. This on-demand model has encouraged binge-watching, where entire seasons can be consumed quickly. That approach suits modern audiences who prefer to immerse themselves in a story without waiting a week for the next episode. It directly responds to how people live and work today, tailoring entertainment options to their unique schedules and preferences.

Affordability plays a significant role as well. Many viewers find subscribing to a handful of streaming platforms more cost-effective than maintaining a full cable package. Even as the number of streaming options grows, consumers still appreciate having the power to choose which services best align with their interests and budgets. This pick-and-choose model starkly contrasts with cable bundles that force viewers to pay for channels they might never watch. Streaming platforms, in turn, have seized user data to refine recommendations, suggesting content that aligns with a person's viewing history. Over time, these personalized experiences keep users engaged and more inclined to maintain their subscriptions.

These factors highlight how a perfect storm of technology, viewer empowerment, and innovative content strategies has propelled streaming into a leading role. It's not just about watching TV anymore; it's about having a versatile platform that caters to diverse needs. With so many titles to choose from and easy access across devices, it's clear why streaming has captured the attention of audiences worldwide.

Opportunities for New Hosts

The shift to streaming platforms has opened doors for aspiring hosts in ways that would have been nearly impossible just a decade or two ago. Traditional television once held a firm grip on who made it onscreen, and getting a foot in the door often meant navigating layers of gatekeepers, from network executives to casting agents. Today, the internet has dramatically lowered these barriers, allowing anyone with a camera and a strong concept to reach a global audience. This newfound accessibility has emboldened creative individuals to produce shows catering to niche interests or overlooked topics, expanding the horizons of viewers' watch.

In the past, launching a show required significant financial backing for studio rentals, professional equipment, and large production crews. The capital needed often pushed independent creators to seek network deals or partnerships, limiting their control over the final product. With streaming, these demands have shifted. High-quality cameras have become more affordable, and robust editing software is now accessible to anyone with a computer. Platforms like YouTube, Twitch, and other streaming services make it possible to publish content without signing contracts or meeting strict network guidelines. This means that whether someone wants to create a talk show about classic cinema or explore the culinary scene in their hometown, there's an opportunity to do so without extensive red tape.

Audiences have also embraced this new wave of content. People grow tired of the same formats and predictable segments often seen on traditional TV, so they actively seek alternative voices that reflect diverse backgrounds, interests, and points of view. This shift in viewer habits has allowed hosts who might never have found support from conventional networks to stand out. They can start small, produce episodes at their own pace, and gradually build a loyal following through word of mouth and social media engagement. Once a show gains traction, hosts can attract sponsorship deals or partnerships that help them refine the quality of their production.

This organic growth was much more difficult to achieve in the era dominated by large television studios.

Another major factor is the direct relationship hosts can now maintain with their audience. Live streaming and social media platforms encourage conversation and feedback, helping creators improve their content and respond to viewer questions or requests. This two-way dialogue fosters a sense of community that traditional broadcasting couldn't quite replicate. The result is a space where hosts can be more responsive, relatable, and genuine—qualities that audiences increasingly value. Rather than being distant celebrities, these new hosts are often seen as friends or mentors, establishing trust through authenticity.

Even established networks are taking note of these evolving trends and seeking fresh talent from online spaces. What begins as a small, self-produced show might catch the attention of larger streaming platforms or production company's eager to invest in new voices. This fusion of traditional and new media highlights how much the industry has embraced diversity in content and the power of grassroots creation. Ultimately, streaming has reshaped the path to becoming a successful host, removing many long-standing barriers and nurturing the rise of more varied, creative, and engaging shows than ever before.

CHAPTER 2

The Role of the Streaming Host

Hosting a show in the streaming era is more than just standing in front of a camera. The individual who takes on this role becomes the guiding voice, the face, and often the creative force behind each broadcast. Audiences look for someone who can offer insights, set a friendly tone, and adapt to the spontaneous nature of live or recorded online content. The responsibilities extend well beyond scripted lines since this modern environment calls for genuine interaction with viewers, even if they're watching from halfway across the globe. A level of trust forms when a host combines knowledge, charisma, and empathy, all while being ready to pivot when a conversation or topic takes an unexpected turn. The rise of streaming has made it possible for these personalities to reach niche communities and massive audiences, transforming the traditional concept of hosting into a dynamic, multi-faceted role that continues to evolve.

You as the Show's Anchor

Stepping into an anchor role means accepting a position beyond simply reading lines or introducing guests. You become the central figure who connects all aspects of the show, guiding viewers through each segment in a natural and engaging manner. As the anchor, you set the tone from when the broadcast begins. Whether you aim for a lighthearted approach, a more serious discussion, or a dynamic blend of the two, your demeanor signals to the audience what to expect and how to engage with the content. This first impression can shape how comfortably viewers settle in, so it's crucial to strike the right balance of warmth, confidence, and authenticity from the outset.

Your responsibilities often begin well before the cameras start rolling. Preparing for an episode involves organizing the flow of content, determining how each segment ties together, and making sure transitions feel seamless. That could mean mapping out an opening monologue, crafting questions for guests, or rehearsing sponsor announcements so they fit neatly into the show's overall structure. In this planning stage, you establish the backbone of each broadcast, ensuring nothing feels out of place. Even if your style leans toward spontaneous conversation, having a roadmap keeps you focused while leaving room for unexpected moments that can make an episode feel lively and unrehearsed.

Once the show begins, you guide viewers from one topic to the next without making them feel lost or disconnected. It's not just about telling people what's coming up; it's about weaving each piece of content into a coherent narrative. If you're discussing a serious subject one moment and a humorous story the next, it's your job to introduce that shift smoothly. This can involve a quick summary of what was just covered, a short personal anecdote to bridge the gap, or an observation that links the two topics together. You maintain momentum that keeps viewers invested in what's happening on screen.

While orchestrating the content flow, you're also setting a welcoming stage for guests who appear on the show. They might be experts, fellow creators, or people with compelling stories. As the anchor, you're responsible for making them feel comfortable so they can share their insights openly. This involves active listening, asking thoughtful follow-up questions, and gracefully steering the conversation back on track if it starts to stray. Your guests' contributions can elevate the program, but the atmosphere you create plays a major role in whether those moments shine.

Above all, your presence should invite the audience into a shared experience. That often means maintaining eye contact with the camera, modulating your voice to match the tone of the discussion, and showing genuine interest in the subjects at hand. It also helps to acknowledge audience reactions when broadcasting live or reading comments on-air. Though it might not seem like a big step, small gestures such as addressing viewer questions or responding to a popular comment can make the audience feel heard. This sense of connection builds trusts, encouraging people to keep tuning in. In embracing these varied responsibilities—preparation, content flow, guest interaction, and audience engagement—you anchor the show in a way that feels both professional and personal, setting the stage for meaningful conversations and memorable moments.

Balancing Entertainment and Information

Delivering a show that captures people's attention while providing valuable insights is an art many hosts spend years trying to perfect. One of the primary challenges is finding the delicate balance between entertaining storytelling and meaningful content. Viewers seek more than simple amusement; they also crave depth, substance, and the chance to learn something new. When you can offer both elements in tandem, you create a richer experience that keeps audiences coming back. The secret lies in structuring your material in a way that doesn't overwhelm with facts yet still satisfies curiosity while maintaining an engaging pace that compels viewers to stay tuned.

Many shows lose momentum when they lean too heavily on data and statistics, presenting them in a dry manner that feels more like a lecture than a conversation. It's easy to get so carried away with sharing knowledge that you forget to add sparks of spontaneity or humor. A balanced approach might include sprinkling facts throughout a segment, introducing each piece with a bit of context, or a brief anecdote that resonates personally. For instance, if you're discussing the popularity of a certain hobby, a short, relatable story about your own experience can pave the way for a deeper look at why the hobby has caught on. This method keeps the facts digestible and the mood personable, reducing the chance that the information will feel like an information overload.

Conversely, relying too much on lighthearted banter and jokes without anchoring them in a larger discussion can make your show feel insubstantial. While humor is often effective for capturing attention, it must serve a broader purpose. Skilled hosts use witty remarks or comedic observations to highlight the significance of a topic, not to distract from it. By weaving humor into the narrative, you maintain a lively atmosphere that points viewers toward the key takeaway. This interplay between levity and seriousness can make potentially complex subjects feel more accessible, as audiences are more likely to absorb information when they're enjoying the process of learning.

Another essential factor is pacing. Rapid-fire delivery of facts can overwhelm viewers, while too much idle chatter risks losing them. Thoughtful transitions between segments allow for moments of reflection, giving the audience time to process what they've just learned before moving on. In a live setting, this might mean pausing briefly to read a comment or acknowledging a viewer's reaction, creating a real-time connection that boosts engagement. During recorded segments, clear signposts at intervals can guide viewers from one point to the next, making the flow feel natural and well-organized.

Trust also plays a vital role. Audiences are more likely to value your information when they trust your intentions and expertise. Demonstrating genuine curiosity about the topic encourages them to be curious alongside you. People respond positively when they feel you're learning with them rather than simply talking at them. This authenticity lays the groundwork for a deeper bond, ensuring that even detailed discussions hold their attention because they sense that you aim to inform rather than perform.

Finding the ideal balance of entertainment and information is a process of continual fine-tuning. By staying aware of your pacing, tone, and level of detail, you can create episodes that delight viewers on a surface level while offering real substance. When done well, this synergy keeps people watching and transforms them into loyal follower's eager to see what you'll explore next.

Connecting with a Virtual Audience

Building a genuine connection with a virtual audience requires a different approach than standing in front of a live crowd. Without the usual cues—such as immediate facial expressions or body language—you must rely on other methods to gauge reactions and keep viewers engaged. Much comes down to trust, authenticity, and shared purpose. When people watch from behind screens, they often seek an environment that feels welcoming and relatable, even though they aren't physically present. One effective technique is to address viewers in a direct yet friendly manner as if speaking with a friend who is miles away. This small change in tone can make a large group of viewers feel like they're each being spoken to individually.

Maintaining eye contact with the camera is one of the simplest ways to foster a sense of intimacy. It might feel awkward initially because there's no live audience to lock eyes with, but looking into the lens gives viewers the impression that you're speaking directly to them. Smiling and using warm expressions also help since emotions get amplified on camera. Even small gestures—like nodding when responding to an imaginary question—can break down the digital barrier, conveying empathy and understanding.

Encouraging real-time interaction makes a difference, even if your show isn't broadcast live. For those who go live, referencing comments or questions from viewers creates a dialogue and reduces the sense of distance. This could involve taking a moment to read a comment out loud, saying the viewer's name, and offering a quick response acknowledging their input. For pre-recorded content, inviting comments and following up in a future episode or on social media keeps the conversation alive. In both cases, the goal is to show viewers that their voices are being heard. People respond positively when they see you're genuinely listening and adapting based on what they say.

Another technique lies in varying tone and pace. Speaking in a monotone voice or sticking to a single style for an entire segment can turn viewers away. By layering in moments of excitement, brief pauses for effect, or gentle transitions into more serious topics, you guide the emotional rhythm of the show. Because you can't watch heads nodding or observe people leaning forward with interest, these speech changes help hold their attention. Viewers subconsciously mirror the energy they perceive, so letting them experience a spectrum of emotions draws them deeper into the content.

Storytelling can also bridge the digital gap. Personal anecdotes and relatable narratives tap into universal emotions, giving viewers a reason to stay invested. If you're discussing complex issues, weaving them into a real-life scenario or illustrating them with a quick story can bring an otherwise abstract topic to life. By making it personal, you grant your audience something concrete to latch onto, fostering empathy and recognition.

Clarity goes hand in hand with connection. Aiming for precision in both speech and visuals reduces confusion. When using images, transitions, or on-screen text, guide viewers through what they see and share how it fits into the broader conversation. Engaging in these small acts of clarity reassures the audience you're committed to making them feel included rather than lost in a sea of information.

Though it may initially seem challenging to engage people you can't see, consistent effort and a personal touch transform virtual viewers into a dedicated community. When each viewer believes they matter as an individual, you build the type of rapport that lasts far beyond a single episode.

CHAPTER 3

Defining Your Show's Concept

A compelling identity for your show sets the stage for everything that follows. By clarifying what you want and how you'll talk about it, you create a roadmap that helps focus both your creative energy and your audience's attention. It's about deciding the essence of your program, capturing the right tone, and defining the unique angle that makes it stand out in a fast-paced digital world.

When that vision is clear, each segment, guest appearance, and production choice aligns with your core idea. Viewers appreciate a show that knows what it wants to be, and that clarity can transform casual watchers into longtime fans. It all begins with a strong concept that resonates with your passion and the interests of the people you hope to reach.

Identifying Your Niche and Audience

Finding the right niche and audience can make the difference between a show that blends into the crowd and stands out with staying power. When you focus your content on a specific topic or community, you tap into an existing need or curiosity that might not be fully satisfied elsewhere. Rather than trying to appeal to everyone, which can dilute your message, narrowing your focus allows you to speak directly to the people most likely to resonate with your ideas. Yet uncovering that sweet spot requires a blend of self-awareness, research, and a willingness to experiment until you hit upon something that feels authentic and needed in the marketplace.

A good starting point is to look at your interests and experiences. When you have genuine enthusiasm for a subject, your passion will shine through every episode, drawing others in. Still, it's important to confirm that other people share that enthusiasm. Online communities can be very telling, whether Reddit groups, niche forums, or social media pages dedicated to a particular subject. By browsing conversations and observing which topics spark the most engagement, you can pinpoint potential areas to explore. It's one thing to guess what audiences want; it's another to see them actively searching for insights, solutions, and new perspectives.

Market gaps often reveal themselves when you notice recurring questions that no one can answer thoroughly or areas where existing shows provide only surface-level coverage. If you keep seeing the same queries pop up, it might suggest an unmet need. At that point, it helps to dig deeper—perhaps by checking keywords on search engines, following relevant hashtags, or paying attention to patterns in viewership data on platforms like YouTube. This methodical research helps confirm that a topic you care about also resonates with a defined, reachable audience.

Once you have a sense of direction, assess the demographics and psychographics of the people who might tune in. For instance, if you're drawn to exploring eco-friendly living, you might target individuals who value sustainability and ethical consumerism. That could include young adults just starting to set up their homes or seasoned environmental advocates searching for new tips. Understanding who they are allows you to shape episodes in a way that speaks their language, addresses their concerns, and meets them where they are in their journey.

Another factor is how accessible your niche should be. Some shows aim at industry insiders, diving deep into technical details that might confuse casual viewers. Others cater to a broader crowd, simplifying complex topics so anyone can follow along. Both approaches can succeed as long as you stay consistent. If you start offering detailed, specialized insights, your audience will expect that thoroughness going forward. Shifting too abruptly could alienate those who have come to rely on you as a trusted source of in-depth knowledge.

Identifying a niche is part art, part science. You match your natural interests and expertise with external data, indicating a demand. Just make sure not to get so caught up in the data that you lose your personal touch. Authenticity remains one of the biggest draws in any form of media, and your ability to connect with viewers on a genuine level can outweigh even the best analytics. Aim for a balance: use research to ensure your subject matter has an audience, then infuse it with your perspective, voice, and experiences. When that alignment happens—when your passion and an audience's needs overlap—a dynamic space emerges where you and your viewers thrive.

Crafting a Unique Value Proposition

In a world where countless shows are uploaded and streamed daily, standing out requires more than solid production values and a charismatic host. The core of any successful program lies in its unique value proposition: the distinctive promise you make to viewers about what they'll gain by watching. This promise is not a mere tagline or slogan. It's a deep understanding of how your show solves a problem, satisfies a craving, or sparks curiosity in a way that others don't. When your concept and execution work together to offer something original, you develop an identity that resonates far beyond a single episode.

Part of this identity hinges on articulating what makes your show different and why that difference matters. You may present a fresh take on a familiar subject, or your show offers a blend of humor and education that feels unlike anything else. It could be as simple as interacting with your audience, creating a distinctive community vibe. The key is to pinpoint an angle that aligns with your passions and expertise, then convey it in a way that instantly communicates why viewers should care.

Clarity is crucial. An overcomplicated or vague concept can lose people before they even press play. If someone scrolls through a streaming platform, they need a concise reason to choose their show over hundreds of others in the same genre. That reason might be rooted in your personal experience—an aspect of your background that equips you to tackle the topic compellingly—or it might lie in the special format you've created. Instead of running traditional interviews, for instance, you might present each segment as a story, walking viewers through a narrative that reveals deeper insights. The clearer you are about this approach, the more likely you will leave a memorable impression.

Audiences often respond best to authenticity, so don't be afraid to lean into what makes you or your perspective unique. If you're particularly passionate about social issues, consider weaving that concern into every episode, adding meaningful layers that spark thought and conversation. Alternatively, if you have a knack for comedy, let that shine through in your commentary or transitions between topics. Consistency in style and substance helps viewers understand that they're in the right place, reinforcing why they clicked in the first place. If they enjoy one episode, they'll know exactly what to expect next time.

It's also important to remain flexible. The streaming landscape evolves quickly, and what worked six months ago might not resonate as strongly today. Keep tabs on your audience's reactions and look for ways to refine or expand your initial concept without losing its essence. This process can involve experimenting with new segments, collaborating with other creators, or asking your viewers for direct feedback. When you listen to audience responses while staying true to your show's core promise, you maintain the fine balance of adapting to viewer needs while preserving your unique edge.

Crafting a unique value proposition blends clarity, authenticity, and adaptability. By identifying what sets your show apart and consistently delivering on that promise, you give people a clear reason to spend their valuable time on your content. In doing so, you create an emotional connection with viewers that encourages them to return and spread the word. This connection can be the deciding factor that lifts your program above the noise in an increasingly crowded streaming world.

Structuring Your Show's Format

Designing the structure of your show involves more than simply deciding how long it should run. Every choice—from segment divisions to episode frequency—contributes to the overall experience you deliver. A well-organized format sets the tone, shapes audience engagement, and maintains viewer interest from start to finish. Each segment or topic can serve as a building block, fitting together into a cohesive flow that keeps people watching and encourages them to return for future episodes.

An effective first step is determining the ideal length for your subject matter and style. Short-form content suits rapid-fire discussions, quick tutorials, or shows targeting busy viewers who appreciate bite-sized entertainment. Longer episodes allow for deeper dives into complex topics, giving you the space to include interviews or more detailed explorations. Both approaches have merit, but matching the duration to the depth of your material is key. If your show tackles intricate issues that need context and analysis, rushing through them in ten minutes could leave viewers feeling shortchanged, and conversely, stretching lighthearted content into extended segments risks losing momentum.

Segmenting your show can help maintain a sense of pacing and variety, which is crucial for keeping your audience engaged. Consider breaking each episode into distinct parts that flow logically from one topic to the next. For example, if your show revolves around food, you might open with a brief story or personal anecdote, move into a recipe demonstration, and wrap up with a quick Q & session. These clear divisions help viewers follow along without feeling lost, and they also simplify your planning process by giving each segment a clear purpose. Over time, this consistency becomes part of your show's identity, letting fans know exactly what to expect.

Audience attention spans can vary based on what they're looking for and how they choose to watch. Some will tune in casually on a mobile device during a break, while others might settle in at home with a longer window of free time. Thinking about your typical viewer's lifestyle can guide episode length and format decisions. It might influence whether you produce short, frequent episodes or opt for more substantial episodes less often. Observing viewer analytics— such as average watch times or drop-off points—can offer insights into how well your structure works. If you see a consistent dip in engagement after a certain time, it might be time to shorten your episodes or shift where you place certain segments.

Frequency is another factor that shapes your relationship with the audience. Posting regularly helps build anticipation and encourages viewers to incorporate your show into their weekly routine. If you opt for monthly specials, you can deliver more polished content that dives deeper into each topic. Consistency in scheduling also signals reliability, showing your audience you take your show seriously. They're more likely to remain loyal if they trust new episodes will arrive on time. Whichever schedule you choose, communicating helps viewers plan to watch or listen, whether they prefer to catch you live or follow up on a replay.

Finally, remember to leave yourself room for occasional changes. The online landscape evolves quickly, and viewer preferences shift just as fast. Stay open to feedback from comments, direct messages, or analytics data. If you notice that certain segments consistently spark more engagement, expand them. If an aspect of your format lags, adjust how you present it or consider replacing it altogether. This combination of planning, analyzing, and fine-tuning ensures your show remains fresh and aligned with the evolving interests of your audience.

Being intentional about length, segments, and frequency sets a firm foundation for a show that feels organized yet flexible enough to adapt over time. This attention to structure improves your content's quality and makes producing episodes that satisfy both creative goals and viewer expectations easier.

CHAPTER 4

Stepping in front of a camera goes beyond delivering lines or memorizing facts. This part of the journey calls for a sense of self-awareness and the ability to connect with viewers sincerely and naturally. It's about conveying who you are, not just what you know. That connection—built on tone, body language, and authentic expression—becomes how audiences remember you. When your voice and presence resonate, they lend warmth and life to any topic you explore, leaving a lasting impression that feels genuine rather than staged. A strong on-camera personality sets the mood for every episode, guiding the viewer's reaction and sparking a deeper level of engagement.

Authenticity vs. Performance

The moment you step before a camera, there's a subtle tug of war between being yourself and putting on a captivating performance. On one side, authenticity allows you to form a genuine bond with viewers. They sense your true personality, pick up your quirks, and trust your reactions and emotions. Conversely, performance can transform mundane moments into something that holds an audience's attention. It involves a heightened sense of presence, deliberate pacing, and carefully chosen words. Striking the perfect balance between these two extremes can be challenging, yet mastering it often marks the difference between a forgettable broadcast and one that leaves people wanting more.

Authenticity is rooted in who you are, including your personal experiences, opinions, and natural communication style. When viewers sense your enthusiasm or curiosity is real, they're more likely to invest in your words. They may start to see you as a companion rather than just a presenter. However, being entirely unfiltered can risk appearing disorganized or unprofessional, especially in a structured show environment. That's where performance skills come in. Learning to refine your natural traits—such as adjusting the pace of your speech or emphasizing particular points—helps you communicate more effectively without losing your genuine spark.

One approach to maintaining this balance is to imagine you're speaking to a close friend who values your knowledge but also appreciates a bit of flair. The friend analogy keeps your tone relaxed and authentic, while awareness of performance elevates your delivery so viewers don't lose interest. Let your genuine humor show through when the moment calls for it, or allow yourself a brief pause to highlight an important insight. This measured performance ensures that key moments carry weight, yet you still sound like your true self. Observing how you come across on camera by reviewing recordings is also helpful. Seeing your facial expressions, gestures, and vocal intonation can reveal whether you're overdoing it or your energy level feels too subdued.

Another important factor is knowing your material well enough to speak confidently without excessive reading or memorization. Adequate preparation reduces nervousness and frees you to respond naturally to unexpected changes, whether a guest's surprising comment or a last-minute technical hiccup. When you're prepared, you can easily adapt, showing the audience your competence and genuine reaction to whatever happens in real time. This ability to pivot smoothly can become part of your performance style—an authentic, human moment that resonates because it's not scripted.

Finding harmony between authenticity and performance is an ongoing process that changes as you develop your skills. Early episodes may feel forced while you learn what resonates with viewers. Over time, you'll recognize which parts of yourself shine most brightly on camera and which presentation techniques genuinely enhance the show. The important thing is to remain open to self-reflection and audience feedback. If something feels off, adjust accordingly, whether that means loosening up and allowing more of your side to show or practicing targeted performance techniques that make your points clearer and more memorable. When done right, this blend of the real and the refined can create a distinctive on-screen presence that draws viewers in, keeps them engaged, and forms a lasting connection they won't soon forget.

VocalDynamics and Energy Management

A strong, consistent vocal presence can transform an ordinary presentation into one that truly captivates viewers. It's more than just speaking clearly; it's about using pitch, pacing, and energy to keep your audience engaged from the first word to the last. Developing vocal dynamics starts with understanding your natural speaking style. Some people speak quickly with a higher pitch, while others have a slower rhythm and a deeper tone. Neither is automatically better, but learning to adjust your voice for clarity and impact lets you keep listeners tuned rather than let them drift away.

Breathing plays a significant role in how confident and steady you sound. Inhaling from the diaphragm, rather than shallowly from the chest, gives you the air support to speak without straining. This method also helps with projection, so you don't have to force your voice to be heard. You can sustain sentences without gasping for breath at inconvenient moments by practicing slow, controlled exhales. Proper breathing technique reduces tension, often appearing in the voice as a wavering pitch or an unsteady tone.

Volume is another tool you can use to emphasize key points. Most of the time, speaking at a moderate level allows you to raise or lower your voice strategically to highlight important ideas or create moments of intimacy. If you constantly shout or remain too loud, your voice can become grating, and the audience will stop paying attention. Conversely, speaking in a monotonous whisper can lull viewers into tuning you out. When done intentionally, shifting between soft and loud keeps people guessing and draws their focus at pivotal points in your talk.

The pace is equally important. Rushing through sentences can overwhelm listeners while speaking too slowly risks boredom. Aim for a rhythm that feels natural but includes occasional pauses, particularly after you've shared a compelling insight. These moments of stillness allow your audience to reflect on what you've said. Pauses also create anticipation as people wonder what you'll say next. This pacing technique can be especially effective when transitioning between ideas or wrapping up a segment.

Tone helps convey emotion and intent. If you speak in an upbeat, lively manner, it suggests enthusiasm, which can be contagious. A calmer tone might be better suited for serious or reflective topics. Whatever the feeling you aim to evoke, consistency is essential. Sudden shifts in mood without reason can confuse viewers and break the flow of your message. Choose a tone that reflects the subject matter, then maintain it, adapting in small increments if the conversation moves to lighter or more serious territory.

Energy management ties all these elements together. While it's important to bring enthusiasm, sustaining it throughout the show is equally crucial. This doesn't mean staying at a high pitch or maximum volume from beginning to end. Rather, it's about pacing your emotional output. If you know you'll be on camera for an hour, plan for moments when you can briefly relax your intensity so you don't burn out. Sipping water between segments or quick mental resets can help you recharge. Viewers will appreciate natural fluctuations in your energy throughout a broadcast, as it mirrors real human interaction better than a forced, unrelenting pep.

You build a vocal style that remains engaging and avoids monotony by fine-tuning your breath control, volume, pace, and tone. This dynamic approach helps you project confidence, showing that you have something worthwhile to say and the skill to say it in a way that resonates. Over time, consistent practice and observation of audience feedback will help you refine your vocal delivery, striking a balance that feels effortless and compelling. When your voice remains flexible and lively, it creates a bond with the listener, ensuring they stay invested in your message from start to finish.

Body Language and Camera Presence

A confident on-screen presence depends on much more than just what you say. How you stand, move, and express yourself visually speaks volumes about who you are and how you want to be perceived. Even subtle gestures can project warmth, enthusiasm, or nervousness. By paying attention to posture, facial expressions, and other nonverbal cues, you can create a sense of ease that resonates with viewers and keeps them engaged.

Starting with posture, standing or sitting upright conveys confidence. Imagine a string attached to the crown of your head, gently pulling you upward. This visualization helps align your spine and relax your shoulders. Slumping forward or leaning too far back can signal disinterest or uncertainty—even if you're feeling alert and excited. When you're steady and balanced, you create a visual that puts viewers at ease. They interpret your composure as a sign that you know what you're talking about and are comfortable being on camera.

Facial expressions play a big role in connecting with your audience. A genuine smile, for instance, can go a long way toward making people feel welcome and at home. It suggests that you're happy to be there and value the time your viewers invest in watching. On the other hand, an expression that's too serious can intimidate or create distance. While a neutral face isn't necessarily a bad thing, it's important to be aware of the message you're sending. If a topic calls for a more serious tone, that should be reflected in your facial cues—but try to keep your features relaxed enough to avoid looking stern. Small changes in your eyebrows or the curvature of your lips can soften your expression, allowing viewers to feel comfortable even if the subject matter is weighty.

Gestures are another critical layer of on-camera communication. Using your hands to illustrate a point can make ideas more tangible, guiding the viewer's focus on what matters. Yet too much movement can become distracting, drawing attention away from your words and onto your flailing arms. It helps to find a moderate range of motion that complements your words without overshadowing them. If you need to convey excitement or urgency, a well-placed gesture can highlight that feeling and invite viewers to share. When a moment calls for calm or reflection, keeping your hands still or lightly clasped can prompt viewers to pause and think along with you.

Eye contact is one aspect of body language that is easily overlooked in a virtual setting. Though you can't see your viewers, maintaining a steady gaze into the camera lens fosters a sense of connection. Even if thousands are tuning in, you're speaking directly to a single person. If you shift your eyes away too often, you risk appearing disengaged or distracted. Practicing by recording short videos of yourself can help you become more aware of where you're looking and how you usually break eye contact. Over time, this practice will help you create the impression of direct conversation, making people feel seen and valued.

The overall goal is to blend these elements into a unified presence. A relaxed posture, genuine facial expressions, and thoughtfully timed gestures support your message. When you're comfortable in your skin, viewers sense it and are more likely to trust what you're saying. Regular practice—reviewing recordings or doing quick rehearsals—helps you fine-tune these nonverbal cues. Eventually, you'll find a natural rhythm reflecting who you are while protecting the best version of yourself on camera. This balance between authenticity and confident communication invites viewers to lean in and truly engage with what you have to share.

CHAPTER 5

Ethical Guidelines and Professional Conduct

Staying true to core values is vital when operating under the public's gaze. Whether speaking to a small group of dedicated fans or a massive global audience, each moment on-screen comes with an added layer of responsibility. It's about more than simply following laws or platform rules—a moral dimension reflects on your character and the trust viewers place in you. You build credibility that can outlast any broadcast by demonstrating respect, honesty, and accountability. Viewers, even if scattered around the world, share a common desire to engage with reliable, thoughtful hosts who treat serious matters with care and lighter moments with integrity. When you uphold respect, fairness, and sensitivity, you create a lasting bond with your audience, proving that entertainment and ethical conduct can go hand in hand.

Setting Ethical Standards

Ethical standards are essential for anyone who appears regularly on a streaming platform. The internet may offer freedoms beyond traditional broadcasting, but it also comes with the responsibility to avoid harmful practices, respect personal and professional boundaries, and ensure accuracy. Viewers often rely on content creators to guide them through complex information or introduce them to unfamiliar topics. When hosts take these duties seriously, they establish a lasting foundation of trust. A reputation for reliability doesn't just benefit a single broadcast—it defines how audiences perceive every word and action.

Respecting boundaries begins with interacting with guests, collaborators, and even the viewers. To create compelling content, it's easy to cross lines that might make others uncomfortable. Before your show begins, let guests know what questions or topics you plan to cover, and be clear about what is off-limits. This openness allows them to feel secure and prepared, reducing any unease that could arise from surprise questions. The same principle applies to footage you might share of others, like bystanders in a public setting. Gaining consent when feasible and blurring faces or details when it isn't shows regard for personal privacy. Even with an enthusiastic audience, pushing someone's limits for the sake of drama can erode your credibility and sow doubts about your integrity.

Avoiding misinformation is equally important. Whether you're discussing health, history, current events, or more niche areas of interest, it's your responsibility to research thoroughly and confirm the accuracy of any statements you make. With so much unverified information circulating online, viewers may come to your show hoping for clear facts or balanced insights. Failing to fact-check can lead to the spread of falsehoods, damaging your reputation in the process. Where appropriate, cite reputable sources or offer direct quotes so people can follow up. If you do make a mistake, correct it promptly and transparently. Admitting an error may initially feel uncomfortable, but most audiences respond positively to honesty. Taking responsibility for inaccuracies is a crucial step in building respect and authenticity.

Closely tied to avoiding misinformation is the need to follow platform-specific content guidelines. Many services outline community standards to protect viewers from extreme or harmful material. These guidelines often address explicit content, hateful speech, or other offensive behavior. Taking the time to read and understand these rules helps you avoid unintentional violations, which can result in penalties like video takedowns or account suspensions. In the long run, compliance ensures your work can remain accessible to the widest possible audience. It also demonstrates that you value a safe and respectful environment for everyone involved, including those who disagree with your perspective.

Another dimension of ethical conduct involves transparency about sponsorships and partnerships. If you're promoting a product or service, audiences deserve to know whether you're being paid for that promotion. Labeling sponsored content or using short verbal disclaimers helps avoid confusion or distrust. People typically don't mind advertisements or promotional segments if they're presented openly. Concealing such deals can breed skepticism, making viewers wonder whether your opinions are genuine or part of a marketing campaign.

Setting ethical standards strengthens the bond between you and your audience. When viewers sense that you care about their well-being, right to accurate information, and comfort level, they become more inclined to support and recommend your work to others. Ethics in streaming is not about stifling creativity or imposing rigid rules on every topic. Rather, it's about creating a space where reliable content, respect for personal boundaries, and transparent practices guide each decision. This approach fosters a healthier online community and builds a legacy that stands the test of time, far beyond individual broadcasts.

Building Trust with Transparency

Fostering trust starts with a willingness to share more than just the final, polished presentation. People want to feel they're not being misled, whether about a product recommendation, a brand partnership, or the behind-the-scenes realities of running a show. By staying transparent, you invite viewers into your process, treating them as informed partners rather than passive recipients of content. This openness safeguards your credibility in a crowded market and enriches the viewer experience, giving them insights beyond what they see on camera.

One of the clearest ways to practice transparency is by being upfront about sponsorships and promotional deals. It's natural for content creators to seek financial support, especially when producing high-quality material that takes considerable time and resources. Yet problems arise when hosts try to camouflage these paid relationships as impartial endorsements. Disguising a sponsor's role can undermine trust, even if the product is solid. A simple statement at the beginning or end of an episode—announcing who has contributed to the show and in what capacity—goes a long way. It assures viewers that you respect their right to understand the motivations behind your recommendations.

Disclaimers can be vital to sponsorship announcements, clarifying that any opinions expressed are your own. This is especially relevant if you delve into health, finance, or legal matters, where misinformation can have serious consequences. A brief, clear disclaimer reminds viewers that your content is for general knowledge, not a replacement for personalized professional advice. It also establishes a framework for accountability. If new information comes to light, you can revisit and revise earlier statements, knowing you've already built a foundation of honesty. Rather than undermining your authority, these clarifications can enhance it, showing you're prepared to adjust and learn.

Behind-the-scenes glimpses often fascinate audiences and build an authentic connection. Sharing bits of your production process—like how you prep for interviews or the methods you use to research topics—breaks down the barrier between you and the people watching. When you admit that certain episodes took extra time to piece together or that you faced unexpected hurdles, viewers gain a sense of your dedication. This transparency breeds empathy and investment, as they appreciate the effort to maintain a consistent schedule or deliver a polished final product. They're also more likely to forgive if technical glitches occur or an upload is delayed.

Maintaining this kind of openness requires mindful communication strategies. Selecting the right moment to talk about a sponsor is crucial—slipping it into a natural break in the conversation is often more respectful than inserting it abruptly. Likewise, disclaimers should be concise and placed so they won't disrupt the show's flow. When you integrate these elements smoothly, viewers understand you take their time and attention seriously. It's about being forthcoming without overshadowing the content itself.

Over the long term, this culture of transparency shapes your relationship with your audience. They learn to expect honesty, and you, in turn, can rely on their goodwill and loyalty. When people feel included and informed, they're more likely to offer constructive feedback, spread the word about your show, and return for future episodes. These benefits can't be measured by a single view count or sponsorship deal; they represent a deeper connection that sets you apart in a competitive landscape. In this sense, transparency isn't just a moral stance—it's also a strategic choice that fosters a vibrant, trusting community around your work.

Handling Controversial Topics and Guests

Sensitive material and challenging viewpoints are inevitable in hosting a show, especially in an era where debates move quickly and passions run high. Presenting controversial subjects can foster meaningful conversations and attract wider interest, but it also carries the potential for heated exchanges or misunderstandings. Setting the right tone from the start helps maintain order and respect. Viewers pay attention to the content of the discussion and how it unfolds, noting whether everyone involved feels heard and whether the host displays fairness. A calm, balanced approach can transform a tense topic into a valuable exchange that sheds light rather than generates friction.

Preparation goes a long way in handling tricky conversations. Before the show, research the background of the issue at hand and any guest with a strong opinion on it. A grasp of major facts, statistics, or common misconceptions allows you to guide the dialogue more accurately. It also positions you to correct misinformation if it surfaces gently. While you may not want to adopt a hard stance, maintaining a basic knowledge of the subject keeps you from getting blindsided by misleading claims. This level of readiness doesn't mean you have to act as an expert on every detail. Rather, it ensures you can ask informed questions and encourage guests to clarify or substantiate their positions.

Framing the conversation at the outset is another effective technique. A brief introductory statement can outline the purpose of the discussion—to explore different sides, highlight ongoing debates, or educate viewers on a complex topic. This helps establish the ground rules for a respectful exchange. You might mention that while strong opinions are welcome, personal attacks or disrespectful language won't be tolerated. Reminding participants and viewers of these expectations creates an environment where differing viewpoints coexist without descending into chaos.

Once the dialogue begins, staying neutral in your moderation style shows that you value every perspective. Neutrality doesn't mean you refrain from asking tough questions; you approach those questions without bias. Encourage guests to support their claims with evidence or examples, prompting them to go deeper into their reasoning. When conflicting views arise, it can help to reflect them in your own words, confirming you understand each side accurately. This active listening technique clarifies points for the audience and signals to guests that you take their views seriously. A gentle interjection—asking each person to pause and consider the other's viewpoint—can reset the tone if emotions start running high.

Maintaining respect involves validating feelings without necessarily endorsing any specific conclusion. You can acknowledge the intensity of someone's belief and even empathize with the roots of that belief, all while avoiding explicit agreement or disagreement. This delicate balance is crucial when dealing with polarizing topics, as it allows everyone to remain engaged without feeling attacked or dismissed. If tensions escalate beyond productive discussion, stepping in with a calming remark or shifting to a brief break helps defuse the situation. This might be as simple as saying, "I appreciate your passion, and I want to ensure we give each viewpoint the time and space it deserves."

After the episode, consider offering a succinct recap or follow-up statement. Sometimes, a summary of key takeaways and a reminder to respect varied perspectives can reinforce the idea that the conversation was meant to foster understanding. Sometimes, you point viewers to resources or direct them to further reading so they can continue exploring independently. By doing this, you uphold your commitment to providing a respectful dialogue space while acknowledging that complex issues can't be fully resolved in one sitting.

Fairness, neutrality, and genuine respect form the backbone of effective discourse around controversial issues. With thorough preparation, clear framing, active listening, and timely interventions, you can transform what could be an explosive debate into an enlightening exchange. These practices enhance the quality of your show and build a reputation for thoughtful hosting that respects both guests and viewers alike.

CHAPTER 6

Show Structure and Scriptwriting

How each episode is organized, and the words chosen to guide viewers can significantly affect how a show resonates. From the moment it begins, a clear plan provides a focus for both the audience and anyone involved behind the scenes. Smoother transitions, well-timed highlights, and a coherent flow help people stay engaged, no matter the subject matter. This planning phase often starts off-camera, mapping ideas out before recording the first frame. When structured effectively, episodes feel lively but never chaotic, blending creativity with consistency to keep viewer's eager for whatever comes next.

Outlining Segment Flow

A well-organized show depends on clear, purposeful segment flow, where every part feels connected to the one before and after. This sense of continuity helps viewers follow along smoothly, regardless of whether the content covers current events, in-depth interviews, or hands-on demonstrations. The opening of a segment serves as the first impression, capturing the audience's attention and setting the mood for what's ahead. Even small details, like a brief teaser or a personal anecdote, can make people lean in and think, "I'm interested; tell me more." Maintaining a consistent style for each new segment is often helpful so viewers quickly recognize that a transition is happening while keeping the energy fresh and welcoming.

Deciding how to open a segment involves considering who's watching and what they expect. When the goal is to spark immediate interest, a lively introduction does the trick—maybe a compelling fact, a short story, or a question that resonates with everyday life. If your content is more educational, a concise topic summary helps viewers understand why the segment matters. In either case, letting your personality come through builds a sense of familiarity. People respond to a host who seems genuinely enthusiastic rather than someone who's simply reading from a script. As you speak, a steady flow and clear voice can further encourage your audience to stay focused and curious about what's coming next.

Transitions can be subtle or bold, but they should always guide viewers from one idea to the next without making them feel lost. A common method is to use a short statement that briefly references the previous topic and then hints at the upcoming one. For instance, if you've just covered a news item, you might bridge to the following segment by saying, "While those developments could reshape our understanding of the industry, there's another perspective we can't overlook. Let's explore how this affects daily life." This type of phrasing ties the segments together under a broader theme, creating a narrative thread. Another approach involves a visual or audio cue, like a short musical riff or graphic overlay, signaling that something new is about to begin. Whether done through words, visuals, or a blend of both, the objective is to keep the momentum going so viewers remain fully engaged.

Closing a segment with intention is just as vital as how you start. A clear wrap-up helps viewers digest what they've just seen, leaving them with a feeling of resolution. Even if you plan to revisit the subject later, summarizing the main points or sharing a final thought offers a sense of closure. A short reflection or a call to action can also be effective. It might be as straightforward as inviting viewers to ponder a key question or encouraging them to share their experiences via comments or social media. By posing a thought-provoking idea right at the end, you give the audience something to remember or discuss. This keeps your content alive in their minds, even after the show moves on to the next topic.

Putting all these elements together—a strong opening, seamless transitions, and a clear conclusion—creates a cohesive rhythm that shapes the entire viewer experience. If each segment feels connected but distinct, your show flows effortlessly from one part to the next. This careful planning also benefits you behind the scenes, making it easier to stay on track and maintain a natural pace. With practice, these transitions will become second nature, letting you focus on delivering great content rather than worrying about how to move from one segment to another. In turn, the audience will appreciate that every moment has been given thought and purpose, giving them a reason to remain tuned in from start to finish.

Balancing Improvisation and Preparedness

Balancing a prepared script with moments of spontaneous creativity can elevate your show from predictable to memorable. Over-reliance on a rigid script might stifle genuine reactions and lead to a monotonous tone, while excessive improvisation can result in disorganized segments and lost messages. The key lies in determining when to adhere strictly to your planned outline and when to embrace the unpredictable energy of unscripted moments. By understanding the value of both approaches, you can harness the best elements of each to deliver a well-structured yet lively program.

Below are key considerations for striking a balance between preparedness and improvisation:

- **Establish Core Talking Points**

Even if you plan to engage in off-the-cuff banter, having a solid foundation of essential topics ensures you don't stray too far from your main themes. Think of these talking points as the anchors that keep each episode on track. When the conversation wanders, glancing at your notes helps you refocus and maintain a coherent flow. This approach also reduces the risk of omitting crucial details you intended to cover.

- **Spot Opportunities for Authentic Moments**

Improvisation often breathes life into a show by reflecting true emotion and real-time reactions. If a guest shares an unexpected story or the live chat sparks a fresh angle on the subject, letting go of the script can lead to spontaneous, memorable interactions. This unpredictability can keep viewers on the edge of their seats. By allowing these unplanned moments to unfold naturally, you capture the excitement that draws audiences in and keeps them invested.

- **Use the Script for Essential Transitions**

While a degree of spontaneity can be refreshing, scripted transitions act as the glue that binds segments together. They ensure that each part of the show feels purposeful, preventing jarring changes in topic or tone. For instance, having a short, well-rehearsed sentence or two to guide viewers from one segment to the next helps create a polished, professional feel. This blend of prepared transitions and live spontaneity maintains a comfortable pace without losing the charm of genuine interactions.

- **Rehearse While Leaving Room for Flexibility**

The best on-camera personalities often run through potential segments in advance, which builds confidence and smooths out tricky wording. However, good rehearsal doesn't mean memorizing every line word for word. Instead, it's about familiarizing yourself with the subject and practicing a fluid delivery. This way, when a fun or unexpected moment arises, you can pivot gracefully without losing your train of thought or stumbling through the rest of the episode.

Preparation also serves as your safety net if nerves get the better of you or if you hit a minor technical hiccup. A detailed outline can help you recover quickly, while a fully memorized script might leave you scrambling if you forget a line. Knowing the gist rather than a verbatim recitation allows you to adapt to unforeseen circumstances, such as an unplanned guest comment or a sudden equipment issue. This flexibility fosters a sense of confidence that viewers can sense and appreciate.

Over time, you'll get a feel for which parts of your show genuinely benefit from a well-defined script—like intros, outros, and sponsor messages—and which segments can thrive on spur-of-the-moment dialogue. The result is a balance that keeps your program organized and vibrant, proving that you respect your audience's time while delivering a performance full of surprises and spontaneity. When done right, this dynamic approach ultimately bolsters your on-air persona, showcasing a mix of professionalism and genuine warmth that draws viewers in and keeps them coming back for more.

Storytelling Techniques

Storytelling holds a special power in any media, allowing viewers to connect more deeply with the content and the person presenting it. Whether hosting a talk show or producing a weekly video series, weaving personal anecdotes, narratives, and thematic arcs into your material can transform dry information into a memorable experience. Stories speak to the human desire for connection. They resonate with personal emotions and lived experiences, inviting viewers to see themselves reflected in your tales. When you approach storytelling with clarity and intention, you can transport an audience into a different world or perspective, all while delivering the core message you want them to understand.

Personal anecdotes work so effectively because they reveal aspects of who you are beyond your expertise. By opening up about a childhood memory, a surprising life lesson, or even a small mishap that taught you something, you let the audience see a more vulnerable, authentic side. This glimpse into your personal history sparks trust because people relate to honest emotions and relatable situations. You may have had an awkward moment during a travel adventure that highlights the importance of stepping out of your comfort zone. Sharing that account shows you can laugh at yourself and learn from your mistakes, which fosters a sense of familiarity between you and your viewers.

To personal stories, building a narrative around each episode or segment keeps viewers engaged from start to finish. A strong narrative has a beginning, middle, and end, even if it's only a few minutes long. The beginning sets the stage; posing a question or dilemma piques curiosity. The middle unravels key details, explores challenges, and builds tension. Finally, the end brings resolution or offers insight, tying together what came before. Treating each segment as a mini story gives your audience a satisfying arc that feels complete yet seamlessly leads into what you'll discuss next. This cohesion helps people follow complex topics without feeling lost, as a logical thread guides them through.

Thematic arcs, which span multiple episodes or segments, deepen the impact of your stories by presenting a recurring idea or motif across your content. You may be focusing on self-improvement, community building, or technological innovation. Each episode can revolve around a specific case study, personal anecdote, or interview that supports that larger theme. Viewers who tune in regularly begin to see patterns emerging, gaining a richer appreciation for the message you're weaving throughout your series. Over time, this approach fosters loyalty as people grow curious about how the overarching storyline will develop.

When using these storytelling tools, authenticity remains key. Trying too hard to force a narrative or exaggerate personal experiences can be insincere. Instead, focus on the elements that genuinely spark your excitement or curiosity. If a certain topic moves you, your enthusiasm naturally shines through, making your stories come alive. Additionally, pay attention to pacing. Too long of a setup can test your audience's patience, while rushing to the conclusion can dilute the emotional payoff. Practice striking a balance, using descriptive language and vivid details without getting bogged down in unnecessary tangents.

Remember that storytelling is a two-way street. Invite your viewers to share their experiences in comments, community forums, or live chats. This creates a feedback loop where stories spark more stories, building a sense of collective understanding. By demonstrating genuine interest in what your audience has to say, you strengthen the connection formed by your narrative. In this way, storytelling moves beyond a single monologue. It becomes an ongoing conversation that leaves everyone feeling more engaged and connected, both to you as a host and to the universal themes at the heart of the tales you tell.

CHAPTER 7

Technical Requirements and Production Essentials

A smooth, engaging show often hinges on more than a good idea and a charismatic host. Behind the scenes, carefully selected equipment and thoughtful production choices shape the viewer's overall impression. From cameras and microphones to lighting and streaming software, each piece works together to create a polished final product. Yet technology can be intimidating, especially for those who are just starting. By taking the time to understand the basic requirements, you gain the confidence needed to troubleshoot hiccups and maintain quality standards. Whether broadcasting from a fully equipped studio or a simple home setup, small, intentional upgrades can make a difference in how your audience experiences every episode.

Equipment 101

Below is a concise overview of the essential equipment for a successful streaming setup—cameras, microphones, encoding software, and internet speed. After the discussion, you'll find a table summarizing the major options to help you compare and decide what works best for you.

A high-quality camera is often the first thing people associate with polished video content. You can start with a simple webcam or a decent smartphone, which are sufficient if you're beginning. As you refine your show or yearn for more creative control, consider upgrading to a DSLR or mirrorless camera. These models allow you to adjust focus, change lenses, and control depth of field, resulting in more professional-looking footage. While the jump in cost is notable, the improvement in picture clarity, especially under varied lighting conditions, can be well worth it.

Just as important as visuals is your audio setup. People are more likely to forgive slightly grainy video than muffled or echoing sounds. If you're on a budget, a basic USB microphone offers a straightforward plug-and-play solution and a major upgrade over a laptop's built-in mic. For those aiming at more advanced production, an XLR microphone connected through a mixer or audio interface opens up sophisticated audio control, letting you fine-tune levels and add effects in real-time. Whatever your choice, remember to position the microphone properly and reduce background noise for crisp, clear audio that keeps viewers listening.

Encoding software translates your video and audio into a format suitable for streaming platforms. Programs like OBS (Open Broadcaster Software) are popular because they're free, versatile, and well-supported by an active community. If you want additional features—such as advanced scene transitions, built-in graphics, or dedicated support—there are paid solutions like XSplit and vMix. The main goal is to pick software that allows you to switch between sources (like different cameras or screen shares) smoothly and manage audio channels effectively. Doing a few test streams before you go live is always wise, helping you spot any lag or sync issues ahead of time.

Finally, your internet speed can make or break a live broadcast. Even the most expensive camera and microphone won't help if your connection constantly drops frames or causes your voice to cut out. A higher upload speed is especially critical for high-definition streams. While recommendations vary, aiming for at least 5 Mbps upload can support 720p resolution reliably. If you want to push 1080p or 4K, you'll need more bandwidth to avoid buffering and stutter. Whenever possible, use a wired Ethernet connection instead of relying on Wi-Fi, as this reduces interference and offers more stable data transfer.

Below is a table highlighting different categories of equipment, from entry-level choices to more advanced options:

Category	Entry-Level Options	Advanced Options	Key Considerations
Camera	Webcam (e.g., Logitech C920)	DSLR (e.g., Canon EOS Rebel) Mirrorless (e.g., Sony Alpha series)	- Resolution & frame rate - Low-light performance - Lens flexibility
Microphone	USB Mic (e.g., Blue Snowball)	XLR Mic (e.g., Shure SM7B) + Audio Interface	Sound clarity - Background noise control - Ease of setup
Encoding Software	OBS (free, open-source)	XSplit - vMix (paid, with extra features)	Ease of use - Scene transitions Community support
Internet Speed	Minimum 3–5 Mbps upload (for SD/720p)	10+ Mbps upload (for 1080p/4K)	Wired Ethernet preferred Consistency of connection - Avoid peak usage times

By examining each category carefully, you can assemble a setup that matches your budget and streaming goals. Upgrades don't need to happen simultaneously; incremental improvements can steadily boost production quality. Start with the most critical pieces—often a decent microphone and reliable internet—then scale up your camera and encoding tools as your show gains momentum. With the right gear in place, you'll be well on your way to delivering a professional, engaging stream that keeps your audience coming back for more.

Creating a Visually Appealing Set

A visually appealing set does more than look nice on camera—it draws viewers in, reflects your show's personality, and signals professionalism. Making thoughtful choices about lighting, background elements, and decorations can transform even the most modest space into an inviting stage. This doesn't necessarily require expensive gear or a full studio setup. Instead, consistent attention to detail goes a long way toward achieving a polished look that keeps your audience focused on you and your content.

Lighting forms, the cornerstone of any attractive set. Even the best camera will struggle to capture crisp images without proper illumination. A soft, even glow can highlight your face and any important props while avoiding the harsh shadows that distract or obscure. Many people start with a simple ring light or an affordable LED panel placed at an angle to soften features and create flattering highlights. Fill lights on either side of the main source to help achieve an even brightness distribution. Some find that bouncing light off a white wall or using diffusers softens it, minimizing glare on reflective surfaces. Natural light can be an asset, too, as long as you can control its direction and intensity through curtains or blinds. Paying attention to color temperature matters as well. Lights marked as "daylight" balance skin tones and produce a more accurate camera hue than warm indoor bulbs, which can cast a yellowish tint over everything.

Background selection also plays a huge role in setting the atmosphere. Something cluttered can pull attention away from the main subject, so aiming for a clean, neutral space often works best. Many creators opt for a plain wall, a bookshelf with carefully placed items, or a fabric backdrop reflecting the show's theme. Colors can set a specific mood; for instance, cool blues and grays add a sense of calmness, while warmer shades provide an inviting feel. Stripes or busy patterns can distract visual artifacts on camera. When showcasing objects behind you, picking items that spark curiosity without stealing the spotlight can enrich the overall aesthetic. This might be a small plant, artwork, or subtle nods to your show's subject matter.

Decorations are a chance to infuse personality into the set, but moderation remains key. Too many trinkets or loud decorations can overwhelm viewers, making them wonder where to look. A few thoughtful pieces representing your interests or aligning with your content's theme can offer just enough visual intrigue. Arranging these decorations at varying heights and distances introduces depth layers, making for a more dynamic shot. Consistency in color and style can help tie everything together, preventing the set from being disjointed.

Practical considerations also influence set design. Clear paths for cables reduce safety hazards and keep your workspace tidy. Minimizing reflective surfaces like mirrors or shiny tables will eliminate random flashes of light or unwanted reflections of your equipment. Whether in a dedicated studio or working from a spare corner of your home, it pays to organize everything so that each episode begins with a camera-ready space.

Bringing these elements together cohesively elevates your show's production quality without requiring an extravagant budget. A little experimentation helps, whether moving lights around to find the most flattering angles or trying different backdrops to see how they appear on video. You create a professional on-screen environment through thoughtful lighting, neat background choices, and simple yet meaningful décor. That visual appeal ultimately draws viewers' focus where it belongs—on you and the story you want to share—while conveying reliability and polish that keep them returning for more.

Ensuring Stream Stability

A great show can unravel quickly if technical hiccups, buffer delays, or audio distortions plague it. Keeping your stream stable isn't just about having high-end equipment; it also requires regular testing, monitoring bandwidth usage, and making informed choices about which platforms to rely on. Putting in the extra effort to solidify these foundations helps you avoid mid-stream chaos and ensures a viewing experience that your audience finds smooth and enjoyable.

At the core of stream stability lies the process of thorough testing. Before going live, dedicate time to simulate your show's conditions: test your lighting, position your microphone, and confirm the clarity of your camera feed. Platforms like OBS or Streamlabs often include built-in test modes that allow you to preview your broadcast without publicly going live. This lets you detect choppy video, out-of-sync audio, or unforeseen background noise. If your schedule permits, a few practice runs can also help you get comfortable with any interactive features or transitions you plan to use. While it's impossible to anticipate every potential glitch, addressing the most obvious issues in advance reduces the likelihood of unpleasant surprises during the show.

Bandwidth management is another critical factor. Even with a fast internet connection, peak usage periods—whether in your household or the broader network—can choke off your upload speeds. If you're trying to stream high-definition content, you'll need a stable upload rate that exceeds the recommended minimum for your chosen resolution. While most streaming at 1080p benefits from at least 5 Mbps upload, pushing 4K video typically requires 15 Mbps or more. Before going live, close unnecessary apps, downloads, or background processes. Opt for a wired Ethernet connection over Wi-Fi if possible since wired connections usually offer more consistent data transfer. Keep an eye on network congestion: if too many devices stream or download large files simultaneously, your show's quality might suffer.

Choosing a reliable streaming platform can also boost stability. Popular services like Twitch, YouTube Live, and Facebook Live have massive user bases, meaning they often have robust infrastructure to handle large traffic volumes. However, if your content caters to a niche community, a specialized platform might be worth exploring—confirm that their servers can handle the level of engagement you expect. Before committing to a platform, review its maximum resolution limits, supported encoders, and any known performance issues. Some platforms also let you enable adaptive bitrates, adjusting your stream quality in real-time if your connection fluctuates. This feature can help avoid total disconnections at the cost of occasionally lowering resolution.

Once you're up and running, monitoring tools provide early warnings when something isn't right. Software like OBS offers real-time indicators of dropped frames and overall stream health, while Twitch and YouTube display live analytics on viewer counts, bitrates, and potential lag. Keeping one eye on these metrics helps you catch small issues before they become major disruptions. If you notice consistent dips, it might be time to reduce your streaming resolution, lower your bitrate, or check for local network interference.

Achieving stability is about preparedness and adaptability. Regular testing, smart bandwidth usage, and a thoughtful choice of platforms provide a strong baseline. From there, monitoring your analytics helps you make quick, informed adjustments. These steps might initially feel technical, but they become a routine part of your production process. Viewers appreciate hosts anticipating common pitfalls and respecting their time by delivering a seamless stream. With that foundation in place, you can focus on content quality, knowing your show will reach the audience in the clearest form possible.

CHAPTER 8

Pre-Production Planning

Putting a show together involves more than turning on a camera and diving straight into the action. Before each broadcast, careful organization lays the groundwork for a smooth, engaging experience. From scheduling guests to gathering all the information you'll need on the day of recording, thorough preparation sets the tone for everything that follows. When all the big and small details are mapped out in advance, everyone involved can focus on bringing their best energy and insights to the stage rather than scrambling at the last minute. This thoughtful approach not only keeps stress at bay but also paves the way for a polished final product that viewers can't wait to watch.

Scheduling and Time Management

Coordinating a production schedule can feel like piecing together an intricate puzzle, especially when guests, collaborators, and audience expectations come into play. Yet these moving parts become far more manageable with a methodical approach. The goal is to outline each step—research, planning, rehearsal, recording, editing—and slot them into a timeline that respects everyone's availability. Finding that balance doesn't just keep the workflow smooth; it also creates a better experience for viewers who rely on consistent releases and a well-polished final product.

A clear starting point is to assess the type of content you're producing. Short weekly segments often demand a fast turnaround, but they can be easier to schedule because each episode requires less prep time. Meanwhile, longer, more in-depth shows benefit from a buffer between shooting and post-production to ensure all components are gathered and edited without rushing. By mapping out these needs early, you establish a baseline that helps everyone involved know what to expect. If you plan to include interviews, knowing the ideal times for your filming or streaming sessions will simplify communicating with potential guests.

Guests may be among the most significant variables in your timeline. People with specialized knowledge or a high profile often have limited windows of availability. Reach out well in advance, ideally with a few options for days and times, so you can land on a slot that works for all parties. A polite, thorough invitation that outlines the proposed topics, the estimated length of the appearance, and the overall goals of the show can encourage them to commit to a date. Once a guest is booked, build the rest of your schedule around that session, from any preparatory research you need to do to final editing and promotion. This approach guarantees that you aren't left scrambling for last-minute details when you're ready to record.

Audience schedules also play a big role, particularly if your content involves live interaction. Observing patterns in viewership data can help you pinpoint the best times to go live or upload a new episode. Some audiences prefer weekends, while others tune in during weekday evenings. If you notice that most of your viewers are online around a specific hour, try to release your content during that window. Over time, consistency cultivates a routine that keeps people returning because they trust that new material will appear simultaneously each week. If your show isn't live, scheduling uploads to coincide with peak traffic can help maximize visibility in crowded online feeds.

Once you've chosen an optimal schedule, keep track of all related tasks using a digital calendar or project management tool. That includes everything from writing scripts and confirming guest details to testing equipment. Setting internal deadlines (like having a script finalized one week before filming) prevents any single phase from sliding off track. If you're collaborating with a team, encourage each member to update their progress so that you can quickly identify potential bottlenecks. When everyone has access to the same timeline, it's easier to avoid confusion over who is responsible for which tasks.

Still, flexibility remains important. Unforeseen events, such as a guest needing to reschedule or an unexpected technical glitch, can disrupt even the best-laid plans. Building a small buffer into your schedule—maybe an extra day for editing or a backup recording date—provides room to adapt without derailing the entire production. Communicating openly with your team and your audience about delays can maintain credibility since people generally appreciate transparency over abrupt cancellations.

Shaping a timetable that accommodates content creation, guest availability, and audience preferences gives your show its best chance to flourish. Consistent uploads foster loyalty, while careful coordination with guests broadens your scope and adds fresh perspectives. As you refine your approach, you'll understand what works smoothly and needs adjustment. Over time, this thoughtful attention to scheduling and time management streamlines the process of making each episode. It strengthens the relationship between you, your collaborators, and the people who tune in.

Research and Preparation

Thorough research and detailed preparation form the backbone of any successful show, helping hosts speak with clarity and confidence. Investing time in gathering information, organizing notes, and rehearsing lays the groundwork for segments that resonate with viewers. This process ensures your content is accurate and engaging while minimizing last-minute stress. Whether presenting discoveries in a field or asking insightful questions in an interview, proper preparation elevates the overall quality of your production.

Effective research begins by identifying reliable sources. The internet holds vast information, but not all can be trusted at face value. It helps to start with reputable sites—official publications, academic institutions, and established news outlets—before venturing into more informal platforms like social media or personal blogs. These alternative sources can still provide valuable anecdotes or perspectives but should be balanced with verified facts. Consider consulting experts or reading peer-reviewed journals if your show focuses on specialized topics, such as health or technology. The goal is to develop a well-rounded understanding of the subject, allowing you to present a balanced view rather than relying on narrow or unsubstantiated data.

Organizing the material, you collect is just as important as finding it. Jotting everything down in a single document can quickly lead to confusion, especially when dealing with multiple segments or guest interviews. Instead, try categorizing your notes by theme or episode section. For instance, you might use headings like "Key Facts," "Controversies," or "Potential Discussion Questions." This structure makes it easier to locate specific details when you're on camera and need to reference a particular statistic or piece of information. Some people also like keeping a separate file or notebook for ideas that don't fit the current episode but may inspire future content.

Writing out a rough outline or script allows you to see the natural flow of your segment before you record. Even if your style leans toward spontaneity, having a roadmap clarifies what you want to cover and how you'll transition between points. Think of it as a guiding framework rather than a rigid, word-for-word plan. This approach allows you to improvise when unexpected moments arise while keeping your content coherent. If you're bringing on guests, share an overview of the topics beforehand so they can prepare relevant points. This leads to smoother interviews and more insightful discussions.

Rehearsing your material instills confidence, especially if you're tackling complicated topics or plan to introduce visual aids. Reading through your outline a few times familiarizes you with the flow, reducing the chance of stumbling mid-segment. Some hosts practice out loud, noting which phrases sound awkward or repetitive. Adjusting them in advance can make your delivery feel more natural. Others like to do a full run-through on camera, then watch the recording to spot areas that need improvement—rushing through key points or missing transitions. By allowing yourself to refine your pacing and tone, you ensure your performance on the recording day is smoother and more polished.

It's also smart to prepare contingency plans if something goes awry. Technical issues, late guests, or forgotten details happen even to the most experienced hosts. If you're ready with backup ideas or alternate segments, you can quickly adapt without losing your audience's attention. This resilience keeps the show on track and demonstrates your professionalism. Over time, you'll gain insight into how much prep is just enough, discovering a balance that prevents you from sounding overly scripted while ensuring you have enough information to be credible.

Research and preparation might take extra time, but they pay off by making your show more informative, cohesive, and compelling. When viewers sense that you've done your homework, they trust you as a source of entertainment and insight. You'll be confident handling in-depth conversations, viewer questions, or live comments without derailing. Ultimately, the effort you invest behind the scenes becomes evident in every segment, reflecting a commitment to delivering a high-quality experience that respects your audience's time and intelligence.

Run-Throughs and Dry Runs

Practicing a show's flow before going live can distinguish between a polished production and one riddled with awkward pauses or fumbling transitions. Even seasoned hosts benefit from run-throughs and dry runs, which offer a controlled environment to test everything from dialogue pacing to technical gear. By simulating the real broadcast scenario, you allow yourself—or your team—to iron out potential snags ahead of time, increasing the odds of a confident, seamless final presentation.

Starting with the content, a run-through helps reveal any clunky spots in your script or outline. You may discover that two segments covering similar points are spaced too closely together, making the content feel repetitive. Or you notice that you're rushing through an important topic and must dedicate more time to it. A rehearsal highlights these weaknesses by forcing you to follow the timeline in real-time. If you're transitioning between segments, you'll see whether the connections feel natural or abrupt. These rehearsals can be as formal or casual as your needs require. Some hosts read through the script solo, imagining how they'd phrase each line, while others gather the whole team—co-hosts, camera operators, producers—to mimic a live setting.

Practicing transitions is especially important when your show includes multiple elements, such as interviews, prerecorded clips, or interactive segments. Shifting from one part of the program to another can be tricky if you don't map it out in advance. During a run-through, notice how you introduce each new part. Are you briefly summarizing what viewers have just seen? Are you giving them a clear sense of what's coming next? A shift that is too abrupt could disorient the audience. This is also the moment to verify that your planned audio or video cues align with your host dialogue's timing. Even if your transitions are more conversational, rehearsals help you see whether that approach feels natural.

On the technical side, a dry run offers a chance to confirm that all equipment works together without glitches. You might discover that the microphone you thought was perfectly balanced picks up background noise or that a camera angle needs adjustment to avoid cutting off someone's head. Lighting can also behave differently once you add motion or switch camera views, revealing shadows or reflections you hadn't noticed. You catch these details in a low-stakes setting by doing a full practice session. It's always easier to fix an issue before the show rather than scramble mid-broadcast.

Internet-dependent elements, like live chat interactions or remote guests, deserve special attention. If you're planning to take viewer questions in real time or interview someone via video call, run a simulated version of those interactions. This allows you to test your internet connection, confirm audio settings, and ensure that screen-sharing or overlay graphics appear correctly. Even a brief test call with your guest can prevent future miscommunication. The better-prepared everyone is, the more relaxed the broadcast feels.

Attitude plays a role in how well run-throughs work. Approaching them with genuine focus sets the tone for everyone involved. If you treat rehearsals merely as an afterthought, small issues might slip unnoticed. On the other hand, scheduling them as an integral part of your production process signals to your collaborators that professionalism matters. Everyone becomes more conscious of timing, clarity, and consistency, which can make the final show sparkle. Rehearsals also build your confidence because you'll have already delivered the material under conditions that closely resemble the real event. This sense of familiarity reduces jitters when it's time to go live.

Finally, remember that even the best dry run can't guarantee a flawless show, especially if you're broadcasting live. Unpredictable elements—like a guest's spontaneous remark or an unexpected viewer question—will always introduce a dash of uncertainty. However, a thorough run-through means you're primed to handle surprises with composure. When you've practiced the foundations repeatedly, small deviations become manageable rather than derailing. In that sense, run-throughs and dry runs act as a safety net, allowing you to adapt gracefully and maintain the flow of your program. Dedicating time to these rehearsals, you help ensure each broadcast reaches its full potential, offering viewers a well-structured, confident performance from beginning to end.

CHAPTER 9

Mastering Interviews and Guest Segments

Having guests on your show adds new voices, fresh ideas, and a layer of excitement that resonates with viewers. Every interview, whether with an industry expert, a rising star, or someone with a heartfelt story, creates an opportunity to explore topics in-depth and connect with audiences more personally. By presenting a thoughtful, comfortable space for conversation, you can uncover perspectives that enrich the overall experience, making each broadcast memorable and worthwhile.

Inviting the Right Guests

Inviting the right guests elevates a show by introducing fresh ideas, expert knowledge, and genuine human stories. The process often involves identifying individuals whose backgrounds or experiences align with your theme. Rather than randomly selecting high-profile names, consider how each potential guest complements the show's direction. If your content focuses on cutting-edge technology, it helps to reach out to people who can discuss recent breakthroughs in a way that resonates with your audience. Likewise, a lifestyle or wellness program might benefit from guests who've made notable strides in health, personal development, or holistic living. Even when aiming for a broad audience, pinpointing guests with focused expertise can offer deeper insights that foster engagement.

Deciding who fits best also involves looking at the breadth of perspectives. Experts can add credibility by drawing from research, real-world data, or years of professional experience. At the same time, influencers or personalities might excel at sharing relatable anecdotes or practical tips that keep viewers entertained. Balancing the two can generate a well-rounded discussion. One guest might offer deep technical knowledge; another could provide a more casual, human angle on the same subject. This variety ensures that segments remain dynamic, appealing to different segments of your audience. Experienced hosts often choose a mix of voices—some widely recognized, others up-and-coming—to keep each episode fresh and authentic.

Research stands as a key step before extending an invitation. Though a person might fit your show's theme at first glance, it's important to dig deeper into their work and public persona. Skim through prior interviews they've done, scan any books or articles they've published, and observe how they interact with their community. This method helps you gauge whether their speaking style and values align with the tone you want to set. You also minimize surprises by ensuring they haven't become associated with controversies that clash with your show's ethics. That said, it's not always about avoiding edgy guests—some controversies can spark meaningful discussions—but you should at least be prepared for those topics if they arise.

When contacting potential guests, clarity matters. A concise invitation highlighting why you believe they'd be a good fit and what they can expect if they join you helps set a positive tone. Let them know the focus of the interview, the approximate length, and any relevant technical details. If you're live streaming, specify the platform and walk them through any requirements, such as camera or microphone setups. The more upfront you are about expectations, the more likely they will feel at ease and ready to share. Setting clear guidelines reduces last-minute confusion, improving the chances of a smooth show.

Considering the audience's perspective further refines your guest list. Consider the questions viewers might pose if they had a direct line to this individual. Would they ask how to break into a certain industry, manage a chronic condition, or balance career and family? By envisioning this dialogue, you can anticipate whether a guest's story or expertise aligns with your audience's wants. This method can also shape how you frame interview questions later on, ensuring the discussion covers ground that feels both relevant and intriguing.

Finally, keep an eye on the long-term picture. While it's tempting to book whichever high-profile person crosses your radar, consistency in guest selection builds a cohesive identity for your show. Audiences often stick around when they sense each episode is part of a larger conversation. As you plan future rosters, consider how new guests can expand on topics introduced by past guests or offer a contrasting viewpoint that encourages deeper reflection. Over time, this thoughtful approach to guest selection establishes a reputation for insightful interviews, drawing viewers who know they can count on each new conversation to spark genuine interest and learning.

Conducting Engaging Interviews

A truly memorable interview hinges on questions that spark thoughtful responses, genuine curiosity from the interviewer, and skillful conversation guiding. Effective hosts understand that people tune in for more than just facts. Viewers want insights into the interviewee's experiences, personality, and perspective. That means going beyond yes-or-no queries. Instead, focusing on open-ended questions prompts deeper reflections and stories, while active listening and gentle direction keep the dialogue on course without stifling natural chemistry.

Developing meaningful questions starts with thoroughly examining who you're interviewing and why. Researching their background, reading articles or watching past interviews, and noting unexplored areas is useful. From there, form broad questions that encourage reflective answers. Rather than "Did you enjoy writing your new book?" you might ask, "What motivated you to explore those themes in your new book?" The latter gives the guest room to describe motivations, challenges, and lessons learned. Open-ended questions function like keys, unlocking personal anecdotes and unfiltered thoughts that can't be neatly wrapped up in a brief "yes" or "no."

Genuine curiosity on the host's part is equally critical. It's hard for the guest to feel enthusiastic about sharing if you're detached or uninterested. When the conversation begins, lean in, maintain eye contact if it's a face-to-face interview, and respond naturally to whatever you hear. If the guest mentions an unexpected detail—maybe they struggled with a particular event or had an "aha" moment during work—seize that opportunity. Ask, "Could you tell me more about what that moment felt like for you?" These spontaneous follow-ups signal that you're truly listening and care about discovering their story's untold sides. An interview that flows from genuine curiosity encourages the interviewee to open up further, often revealing insights that a tightly scripted set of questions would never uncover.

Active listening involves more than just waiting your turn to speak. As the guest responds, please consider their voice, expressions, or body language nuances. Are they excited, tense, or hesitant? If you sense discomfort, gently steer the conversation toward a safer space, but if they seem eager to continue, invite them to expand on the topic. Echoing or paraphrasing certain points shows that you understand and value what they say. For instance, if a guest describes a challenging childhood experience that shaped their career, you might reply, "So that period pushed you to prove yourself, which ultimately led to your breakthrough?" This reflective approach reassures them that their story is being heard and processed.

Guiding the conversation means balancing these immersive, unpredictable moments with a degree of structure. While an interview should feel natural, you likely have key topics or segments you aim to cover. Gently bringing the guest back to these points—especially if they wander into tangential subjects—keeps the session cohesive. A smooth redirection might start with a supportive phrase like, "That's fascinating. It reminds me of something I read about your work. Could we talk about how you first discovered this passion?" This approach bridges their latest remark with a more focused direction. It doesn't abruptly cut them off or disregard what they've been sharing; it simply nudges the conversation to the next area you'd like to explore.

Successful interviews strike a balance between structured planning and organic discovery. Open-ended questions lay the groundwork, but genuine curiosity and active listening add depth and spontaneity. A skilled interviewer knows when to follow a guest down an unexpected path and when to guide them toward planned talking points. This dance of free-flowing dialogue and gentle direction creates an atmosphere of trust, encouraging guests to share thoughts and experiences they might not reveal under less attentive questioning. Over time, honing these skills leads to richer, more enlightening conversations that viewers remember long after the episode ends.

Overcoming Surprises

Unpredictable moments can inject energy and tension into any interview or panel discussion. When guests steer the conversation off course, or hot-button issues unexpectedly come up, it's easy to feel thrown off. However, keeping your cool and skillfully managing these twists can elevate your show's quality. By responding with measured poise rather than panicking, you demonstrate confidence and help maintain a respectful environment that encourages genuine dialogue. Over time, learning to adapt to these high-pressure scenarios can become one of your strongest assets as a host.

A key principle is to remember that your role involves guiding the conversation, not controlling it entirely. Real people can't be scripted, even if you've planned a detailed structure for the episode. They may share stories that seem unrelated to the topic or inadvertently push sensitive buttons. Instead of shutting them down too abruptly, listen for potential links to your primary theme. Sometimes, guests wander onto tangents that, if reframed, connect back to the original subject in fresh and interesting ways. If their comments appear completely unrelated, interject politely once they finish a thought: "That's quite insightful—how does that experience tie back to your work?" This subtle steering recaptures the main focus without undermining the guest's perspective.

When controversies surface, your job is to keep the dialogue constructive. Viewers often appreciate shows that can tackle tough or divisive subjects with maturity. Consider acknowledging that the topic is complex and offering a quick summary of differing viewpoints so the audience understands the broader context. Then, invite your guest to elaborate on why they hold their opinion, encouraging them to cite experiences or evidence that shaped their stance. This approach frames the conversation as an exploration of viewpoints rather than a clash of personalities.

Maintaining composure also involves letting go of the need to have all the answers. If a guest challenges you with unfamiliar data, be honest about it. "I'm not familiar with that study—could you elaborate?" or "I'll have to look into that further" are valid responses. Admitting you don't know something isn't a weakness; it's a sign of integrity. Embracing a curious attitude prevents the discussion from devolving into a defensive back-and-forth. If a real disagreement emerges, guide the conversation toward constructive ground. For example, say, "It sounds like we have different perspectives based on our experiences—what do you think we can learn from each approach?" This question invites collaboration rather than confrontation.

Occasionally, guests may use strong language or make unexpected statements that are inappropriate or offensive. While you want to allow candid dialogue, setting boundaries that align with your show's values and any platform rules is crucial. If a remark crosses a line, calmly address it at the moment: "I understand you have strong feelings here, but I'd like to keep our language respectful for our viewers." Don't hesitate to remind guests of guidelines if they push too far. Most guests will appreciate clear communication, and viewers will note your firm yet professional stance.

Another way to handle sudden tensions is through short, strategic breaks. If an emotional conversation becomes heated, briefly pause for a sponsor message, a musical interlude, or a simple transitional statement. This break lets everyone breathe, gather their thoughts, and continue with a clearer head. Once the segment resumes, you can summarize the issue, helping everyone refocus on the core debate rather than tangential disputes.

Be prepared to reflect after the episode ends. Review how you handled the guest's deviations or the unexpected controversy, and consider what worked well versus what felt forced. This feedback loop strengthens your hosting abilities over time. Each twist in the conversation becomes an opportunity to refine your approach, enhance your flexibility, and build the kind of credibility that comes from confidently handling whatever surprises come your way.

CHAPTER 10

Fostering Audience Engagement

Connecting with viewers goes beyond just letting them watch. A deeper, more meaningful bond forms between the creator and the audience by actively involving them in real-time or encouraging ongoing participation. In this interactive environment, listeners or viewers feel seen, heard, and valued, which can turn casual fans into loyal followers. Every moment spent responding to comments, asking for input, and adapting content based on feedback boosts interest and fosters a sense of community. When people know their voices matter, they're more likely to stay tuned, share the experience with friends, and keep returning for more.

Live Interaction Techniques

Incorporating live interaction techniques into your show can significantly enhance viewer engagement, transforming passive audiences into active participants. Techniques like utilizing chat features, conducting polls, and hosting Q&A sessions make the viewing experience more interactive and strengthen the community around your content. By integrating these elements effectively, you can foster a dynamic environment where viewers feel connected to the content, each other, and you as the host.

Utilizing Chat Features

Many streaming platforms offer live chat capabilities, allowing viewers to comment in real-time as they watch. Engaging with this feature effectively can greatly enhance the live experience. As a host, acknowledging comments, answering questions, and reacting to viewer input during the broadcast can make your audience feel heard and valued. You might highlight interesting comments, offer shout-outs, or use viewer suggestions to steer the conversation. This direct engagement keeps the audience involved and adds a layer of spontaneity and personalization to your content.

However, live chat can be overwhelming, especially with a large audience. Employing a moderator can help manage the flow of comments, filter out inappropriate content, and highlight questions or contributions that are particularly engaging or relevant. This helps maintain a respectful and constructive discussion environment, ensuring that the chat enhances the show rather than distracts from it.

Conducting Polls

Polls are a powerful tool for interactive engagement. They provide a quick way for viewers to voice their opinions and influence the direction of the discussion or the content itself. For example, you could use polls to decide topics for future episodes, choose between segments, or gather opinions on issues discussed during the show. This makes viewers feel like they are part of the content creation process and gives you valuable insights into your audience's preferences and interests.

Polls can be integrated directly into many streaming platforms, or you can use third-party tools that link to your broadcast. Displaying real-time results can add excitement and a sense of immediacy, keeping the audience hooked as they see the impact of their participation unfold live.

Hosting Q&A Sessions

Q&A sessions are a direct and structured way to engage with your audience, allowing them to ask questions about you, your guests, or the topics covered. These sessions can be held at the end of a show or as standalone episodes, providing an excellent opportunity for deeper interaction. To maximize their effectiveness, promote your Q&A sessions ahead of time, encouraging viewers to submit questions through social media or directly on the streaming platform. This builds anticipation and ensures that you have diverse questions to address during the session.

During Q&A, be responsive and thoughtful. Taking the time to give well-considered answers shows that you respect your audience's curiosity and viewpoints. If you cannot answer all questions during one session, you might follow up in subsequent episodes or through social media posts, keeping the conversation going and maintaining viewer interest.

Effectively utilizing chat features, conducting polls, and hosting Q&A sessions are key strategies for fostering audience engagement in a live setting. These techniques encourage viewers to participate actively in your broadcast, contributing to a lively, interactive community around your content. By making your audience a central part of the experience, you enhance their enjoyment and investment in the show and build a loyal following that will likely grow over time.

Building an Online Community

Building an online community around your show extends the conversation beyond the broadcast itself, creating a vibrant ecosystem where viewers can interact, share, and contribute. This continuous engagement fosters a sense of belonging and loyalty, turning casual viewers into active community members. Key strategies such as encouraging user-generated content, hosting forums, and maintaining a strong social media presence are essential in cultivating this environment.

Encouraging User-Generated Content

User-generated content (UGC) is a powerful way to involve your audience directly in the creative process. This could be as simple as asking viewers to submit their videos, photos, stories, or artwork related to your show's themes. For instance, if your show covers DIY projects, you could encourage viewers to share their projects using a specific hashtag. Not only does this provide content that you can feature in your episodes, but it also gives your audience a platform to showcase their skills and creativity. This inclusion can make fans feel appreciated and valued, reinforcing their connection to your brand.

To maximize participation, offer incentives for sharing content, such as featuring the best submissions on your show, offering prizes, or even giving shoutouts. Clear guidelines on how to submit content and what types of content are acceptable are crucial to ensure that all contributions enhance the community experience.

Hosting Forums

Online forums or discussion boards can be a gathering place for your audience to discuss episodes, share ideas, and provide feedback. These platforms allow for deeper discussions beyond social media comments' limitations. They can be hosted on your website or through third-party services supporting community engagement.

Managing a forum requires setting clear rules about conduct to ensure discussions remain respectful and constructive. Regular participation from you or your team can guide conversations, answer questions, and moderate discussions to keep the community healthy and active. Engaging directly in the forums also shows that you value your audience's thoughts and are committed to being part of the community, not just the face of the show.

Maintaining a Social Media Presence

Social media platforms are invaluable for building and maintaining an online community. They provide a space to share updates, tease upcoming content, and interact directly with viewers. Each platform has unique strengths—Instagram is great for visuals, Twitter for quick updates and conversations, and Facebook for longer posts and community groups.

Consistency is key in social media management. Regular posts keep your show at the top of your mind, while responsiveness encourages interaction. Engage with comments, share posts from community members, and participate in relevant conversations. Additionally, live social media events, like Q&A sessions or live tweets during broadcasts, can create real-time engagement opportunities.

Social media analytics can offer insights into what content resonates most with your audience, allowing you to tailor your approach based on real data. This responsiveness to audience preferences improves engagement and helps you refine your overall content strategy.

Building an online community is about more than just broadcasting content—it's about fostering an ongoing dialogue that enriches the viewer's experience. You create a multifaceted platform where viewers can become active participants by encouraging user-generated content, hosting forums, and engaging on social media. This engagement transforms passive audiences into a dynamic community, driving loyalty and making your show a meaningful part of their daily lives.

Feedback Loops

Establishing effective feedback loops is crucial for any show's continuous improvement and relevance. By actively seeking and analyzing viewer feedback, creators can adjust their content to meet audience needs and preferences better, enhancing engagement and satisfaction. This ongoing refinement process helps ensure your show remains dynamic, responsive, and tightly connected to its audience base.

Gathering Viewer Opinions

The first step in creating a robust feedback loop is to collect viewer opinions. This can be achieved through various methods, each offering different insights. Surveys and polls, for instance, are great tools for obtaining structured feedback. They can be easily distributed via email newsletters, embedded on your website, or shared through social media. Surveys can ask specific questions about what viewers like or dislike, what new topics they're interested in, or how they feel about the show's format and presentation.

Another effective method is monitoring comments on social media and video platforms where your content is posted. Comments often provide more spontaneous and honest feedback, as viewers will likely share their immediate reactions and thoughts. Additionally, hosting live Q&A sessions can encourage direct interaction, where viewers feel they actively participate in the show's development.

Analyzing Comments

Once feedback is gathered, the next step is analysis. This involves sifting through the data to identify common themes and patterns. Are there particular segments or topics that consistently receive positive or negative reactions? Do viewers express a desire for more depth or diversity in the content? Analyzing this feedback allows you to pinpoint areas of strength to build upon and weaknesses that need addressing.

It's important to approach this analysis with an open mind and a willingness to adapt. While not all feedback will be actionable or relevant, constructive criticism should be welcomed and considered carefully. This might involve making adjustments such as altering the pacing of episodes, introducing new formats, or even changing the visual aesthetics of the show.

Refining the Show

The ultimate goal of gathering and analyzing feedback is to refine your content. This iterative process should be integrated into your show's production cycle. After implementing changes based on viewer input, observe how these adjustments impact engagement and satisfaction. Do the changes lead to more positive comments, increased viewership, or higher viewer retention rates?

Continuously refining your show based on feedback also involves experimenting. Sometimes, the audience's suggestions may lead you in new directions that require trial and error. Communicating these changes to your audience is crucial, letting them know their input has been heard and is valued. This fosters a sense of community and encourages more feedback, creating a healthy cycle of improvement.

Additionally, it's beneficial to highlight when specific changes have been made because of viewer feedback. This can be done through shootouts during episodes, community forum updates, or social media posts. Such acknowledgments validate the audience's contribution and reinforce the participatory nature of your show.

Effective feedback loops are essential for any show that aims to maintain and grow its audience. By systematically gathering, analyzing, and acting on viewer feedback, you can ensure your content remains relevant and engaging. This improves the show's quality and strengthens the relationship between you and your audience, setting the stage for sustained success.

CHAPTER 11

Marketing and Promotion

No matter how great a show is, it needs visibility to attract and retain an audience. Marketing and promotion ensure that content reaches the right viewers and gains traction over time. A well-thought-out strategy helps build anticipation before episodes' air, keeps engagement high between broadcasts, and expands the show's reach beyond its initial audience. By leveraging various promotional techniques, from social media campaigns to collaborations with other creators, a show can steadily grow its following and establish a lasting presence in the competitive world of streaming entertainment.

Marketing Promotions and Advertising

Marketing a streaming TV show hinges on blending creativity with strategic planning. Every promotional effort—from online ads to public relations—should highlight what sets the show apart while reaching viewers likely to engage with its content. Knowing the core demographic is crucial, since successful campaigns speak directly to a group's interests, values, and viewing habits. A family-friendly show might emphasize heartwarming moments and feature bright, upbeat visuals; a suspenseful drama could rely on moody color palettes and more intense messaging.

Brand consistency amplifies recognition. Viewers can sense when the same tone, style, and visual cues appear across social media, trailers, and interviews. This coherence not only builds trust but also sets the show's identity in a crowded marketplace. Crafting promotional videos like teasers and trailers becomes an exercise in storytelling, using short bursts of footage and compelling narration to instill curiosity. Audiences who watch these clips should leave with a clear idea of the show's essence, eager to tune in.

Budgeting decisions revolve around goals and available resources. Some productions invest heavily in a high-profile launch strategy, seeking immediate buzz. Others take a slower approach, spreading funds over weeks or months to maintain steady visibility. Media buying involves selecting the most effective platforms—social media ads, podcast sponsorships, or influencer shoutouts. Each option has unique benefits: targeted digital ads can filter audiences by demographic or interest, while influencer partnerships often deliver authentic endorsements that resonate with loyal followers. Cost varies, so setting clear metrics helps creators gauge whether an ad spend is worthwhile. For instance, tracking click-through rates and sign-ups from a specific sponsored post reveals how effectively the message converts viewers into fans.

Flexibility matters, too. Monitoring how audiences respond—through comments, likes, shares, and new subscribers—offers insights on what works. If Instagram posts receive high engagement, shifting more resources toward that channel can maximize impact. Collaborations with creators or brands whose identities align with the show's themes can further extend reach. A cooking series might partner with a renowned chef, while a fantasy show could team up with a cosplayer or gamer who shares a passion for imaginative storytelling.

Timing also plays a role. Scheduling a promotional push around a premiere, finale, or special event can boost viewership. Launching at times when competition is low may help a series stand out. Meanwhile, ongoing engagement strategies—like behind-the-scenes content or interactive live streams—keep fans invested beyond a single marketing spike, creating word-of-mouth momentum that money alone can't buy.

Effective marketing for a streaming TV show requires honing a clear voice, carefully choosing channels, and constantly learning from the audience. The right combination of distinctive branding, targeted outreach, and flexible adaptation can transform a new or niche series into must-see viewing, even in a marketplace saturated with options. When viewers feel that a show speaks to them personally—and see evidence of high-quality production—they are far more likely to commit their time, spread the word, and follow each new development in the story.

Social Marketing and Public Relations

Social marketing and public relations are often the backbone of a successful streaming TV show's promotional campaign. While social platforms create direct connections with viewers, a robust PR strategy increases credibility, media coverage, and industry recognition. When executed effectively, these tactics work together to form a dynamic system of engagement that not only piques initial interest but also sustains enthusiasm over time. Below is a closer look at how social marketing and public relations can elevate a show's profile and build an enduring audience.

Leveraging Social Platforms

Social media has reshaped how audiences discover and discuss entertainment. Platforms such as Instagram, TikTok, Twitter, and LinkedIn each serve distinct demographic groups and offer unique opportunities for interaction. Understanding the core purpose and culture of each platform is key to maximizing engagement:

Instagram stands out for visual storytelling. Hosts and producers can share behind-the-scenes photos, short clips, and stories that allow followers to see the creative process. High-quality images or engaging reels featuring cast highlights, set details, or sneak peeks can generate excitement. Additionally, live sessions on Instagram allow for real-time Q&A, bridging the gap between creators and fans.

TikTok specializes in snappy, entertaining videos that can go viral if they hit the right note. Teasers, bloopers, or short comedic segments related to the show can fit perfectly into TikTok's format. This platform appeals strongly to younger audiences and thrives on trends, so integrating viral challenges or hashtag campaigns can significantly broaden reach.

Twitter excels at real-time dialogue. Quick updates, witty observations, and polls can engage followers around ongoing show developments or episodes as they air. Twitter's conversational nature also makes it ideal for live-tweeting premieres or finales, fostering a communal viewing experience.

LinkedIn may seem like an outlier, but it serves a valuable role if the show targets business professionals or more industry-focused content. Posting production updates, sharing thought leadership articles related to the show's subject matter, or announcing professional milestones—such as partnerships or speaking engagements—can help creators connect with an audience beyond traditional entertainment circles.

A coherent strategy involves consistent posting, brand alignment, and active community management. Responding to comments, liking fan posts, and acknowledging user-generated content build loyalty. Short-term campaigns, such as countdowns to a premiere, can drive immediate excitement, while ongoing social engagement fosters sustained interest between major announcements or episode releases.

Building a PR Strategy

While social media builds direct lines of communication with fans, public relations initiatives broaden the show's visibility across conventional and digital media outlets. A structured PR plan positions the show for features, interviews, and mentions that lend credibility and attract new viewers.

Crafting Press Releases: A well-written press release can catch the eye of journalists, editors, or bloggers. It should lead with a concise, compelling hook—perhaps a notable angle, a captivating storyline, or a partnership with a high-profile individual. Details about the show's launch date, cast, and production background follow. Including quotes from creators or cast members adds personality to the release, making it more interesting to potential readers. Formatting with clear headers, bullet points for key data, and straightforward language helps busy journalists quickly grasp the main points.

Pitching to Media Outlets: Direct outreach to relevant publications can secure interviews, reviews, or feature articles. Tailoring each pitch is crucial: an entertainment magazine might want an exclusive interview with the lead actor, whereas a technology site could be more interested in the innovative filming techniques used. Personalized emails that reference the outlet's style or previously covered topics show genuine interest and increase the odds of a positive response.

Managing Interviews and Appearances: Once outlets agree to cover the show, effective coordination ensures consistent messaging. Sharing a simple document with talking points, background details, and interesting anecdotes helps participants in interviews stay aligned. Creators who appear on podcasts, radio shows, or live panels benefit from rehearsing succinct ways to describe the show's premise and its unique appeal. Keeping a friendly yet professional tone builds trust with both hosts and audiences.

Expanding Visibility and Credibility: When journalists or influencers praise a show, quoting these endorsements on social media, in trailers, or on promotional materials can enhance credibility. Collecting snippets from positive reviews—often referred to as "pull quotes"—provides a quick, impactful way to convey the show's reception. If well-known publications or respected critics weigh in, referencing their enthusiasm can sway new viewers who value external opinions.

A successful PR strategy thus complements social marketing by reaching audiences who may not be active on platforms like TikTok or Instagram. Traditional press coverage (including digital news sites and TV interviews) still carries significant weight, particularly for older viewers or niche audiences who rely on trusted journalistic voices. Moreover, mainstream media mentions frequently circulate online, fueling additional social media shares and discussions, which further amplifies reach.

Together, social marketing and public relations create a comprehensive approach to building momentum for a streaming TV show. Social platforms let creators converse with fans in real time, share exciting visuals, and adapt content to viewer responses. PR work, meanwhile, taps into professional networks and media channels, adding external validation that can win over more skeptical audiences. By integrating both tactics, a show maximizes its potential for meaningful engagement, growing a fanbase that sees value in not only the content itself but also the community and credibility surrounding it.

Branding Your Show

Branding gives your show a distinct identity that is instantly recognizable to viewers. A strong brand creates an emotional connection with your audience and sets expectations for what they can anticipate from your content. While great storytelling and engaging topics keep people coming back, the right visuals, taglines, and overall aesthetics play a crucial role in capturing attention in the first place. When executed well, branding makes your show look professional and strengthens its presence across platforms, helping it stand out in an increasingly crowded digital space.

One of the most important elements of branding is your logo. A well-designed logo serves as a visual signature, representing the tone and personality of your show. Whether bold and dynamic or sleek and minimalist, your logo should reflect the essence of your content. For example, a technology-focused show might use sharp, futuristic fonts and cool-toned colors, while a lifestyle or wellness program might lean toward softer, more inviting hues. Simplicity is key—an overly complex design can become difficult to recognize at smaller sizes, such as profile pictures or video thumbnails. A memorable, scalable logo ensures consistency across different platforms, from your website to social media and promotional materials.

Equally important is the **tagline**—a short, catchy phrase that encapsulates your show's purpose or appeal. A great tagline gives potential viewers a quick idea of what they can expect. Think of iconic phrases like "The world's news, made simple" or "Where science meets storytelling." A tagline should be concise yet meaningful, helping to reinforce your brand identity in just a few words. When brainstorming, consider what makes your show unique. Is it the depth of your analysis, humor, or the personal perspective you bring? Incorporate that essence into your tagline to make it descriptive and memorable.

Beyond the logo and tagline, the visual style of your show should be carefully crafted to maintain consistency. Colors, typography, and graphics all contribute to a cohesive brand image. Choosing a primary and secondary color palette helps unify all visual elements, from video thumbnails to social media posts. Similarly, selecting one or two fonts for all promotional materials ensures a professional look. If your show includes on-screen graphics, lower thirds, or animated intros, they should align with the overall aesthetic rather than feeling like separate, unrelated components.

Thumbnails and cover images play a major role in attracting viewers. People often make snap decisions based on visuals when scrolling through content. Eye-catching, well-branded thumbnails help increase click-through rates and reinforce familiarity. Using consistent color schemes, logo placements, and text overlays can make your content easily identifiable, even at a glance.

Another aspect of branding is your on-camera presence. Whether you're hosting solo or featuring guests, how you present yourself should align with your established brand image. If your show has a casual and relatable tone, your style and setting should reflect that. A structured backdrop and formal delivery might be a better fit if it's more polished and informative. Consistency in how you appear helps reinforce the identity of your show, making it more recognizable to returning viewers.

Ultimately, branding is about more than aesthetics— creating an experience that resonates with viewers. By developing a strong visual identity, a compelling tagline, and a consistent presentation style, you ensure that your show is engaging and leaves a lasting impression. A well-branded show builds trust, loyalty, and recognition, all contributing to long-term success in an ever-evolving digital landscape.

Cross-Platform Promotion

Expanding your show's reach requires more than just uploading episodes and hoping for an audience to find them. Cross-platform promotion strategically engages viewers across different spaces, ensuring your content reaches new audiences while keeping existing fans engaged. By sharing teasers on social media, repurposing content for YouTube, and collaborating with other creators, you maximize visibility and give people multiple entry points to discover your show.

One of the most effective ways to generate interest is by sharing teasers and highlights on social media. Short, engaging clips from your show preview what viewers can expect, sparking curiosity and encouraging them to watch the full episode. Platforms like Instagram, Twitter,

Facebook, and TikTok thrive on quick, eye-catching content, making them ideal for sharing bite-sized moments that hook potential viewers. These clips should capture intriguing moments—a thought-provoking quote, an emotional reaction, or a funny exchange. Adding captions ensures accessibility and makes it easier for users scrolling through their feeds to engage without sound. Posting behind-the-scenes footage or countdown reminders before a new episode airs also helps build anticipation.

Leveraging YouTube clips and repurposed content is another powerful way to extend your reach. While full episodes might be hosted on a streaming service, breaking them down into smaller segments allows audiences to engage with your content in a more digestible format. If an episode features an insightful discussion, a powerful guest moment, or an entertaining debate, extracting that portion and uploading it to YouTube can attract viewers who might not commit to watching an entire show immediately. These clips can also be evergreen, generating views long after the original broadcast. Optimizing video titles, descriptions, and thumbnails helps boost search visibility, making it easier for new viewers to find your content when looking for related topics.

Collaborating with other creators introduces your show to new audiences while adding variety to your content. Partnering with influencers, industry experts, or fellow content creators can take different forms, from guest appearances to cross-promotional shoutouts. When selecting potential collaborators, look for those whose audience overlaps your target viewership. If their followers enjoy similar content, they will likely check out your show. A guest episode where both creators promote the content to their respective audiences can lead to substantial growth. Social media takeovers or joint live streams also create interactive moments that engage both audiences simultaneously, strengthening community ties.

Engagement doesn't end after promotion; maintaining an active presence across platforms helps keep your audience invested. Responding to comments, resharing user-generated content, and participating in trending conversations related to your niche keep your show relevant between episodes. Encouraging viewers to share their thoughts and spread the word creates organic promotion, as fans naturally introduce the content to their circles.

Cross-platform promotion is ultimately about meeting audiences where they are. Not everyone consumes content in the same way, so repurposing and strategically sharing your material across multiple platforms increases the chances of reaching people who may not have otherwise discovered your show. By creating a consistent presence across different digital spaces, you expand your reach and establish a stronger, more engaged community that continues to grow over time.

Growing Organically vs. Paid Advertising

Building an audience for your show requires a strategic mix of organic growth and paid advertising. While organic methods—such as word-of-mouth, social media engagement, and content optimization—help establish trust and long-term loyalty, paid ads can accelerate exposure and reach new viewers quickly. Striking the right balance between these approaches ensures steady, sustainable growth while maximizing promotional opportunities.

The Power of Organic Growth

Organic growth relies on natural audience expansion through content quality, community interaction, and share ability. One of the most effective organic strategies is word-of-mouthmarketing. When people genuinely enjoy a show, they recommend it to friends, post it on social media, or engage in discussions. Encouraging this process by creating highly shareable moments—funny clips, deep insights, or emotionally resonant scenes—helps attract new viewers. Additionally, prompting existing followers to tag others, leave comments, or share their favorite episodes fuels organic visibility.

Social media plays a critical role in organic discovery. Regularly posting engaging content, responding to comments, and joining conversations within your niche keeps your show circulating. Hashtags, collaborations, and interactive posts (like polls or Q&A sessions) encourage participation and help extend your reach. Platforms reward active engagement by making highly interactive posts more visible to a wider audience.

Another key factor in organic growth is search engine and platform optimization. Using relevant titles, descriptions, and tags on YouTube improves discoverability, as does maintaining a consistent posting schedule. Strong branding, eye-catching thumbnails, and strategic episode descriptions on streaming services attract casual browsers. Even embedding episodes into blog posts or partnering with websites that align with your content can drive long-term traffic.

Despite its long-term benefits, organic growth can be slow. It requires patience and consistency before noticeable results appear. That's where paid advertising can provide a boost.

The Role of Paid Advertising

Paid promotions help reach audiences who might not otherwise come across your show. Platforms like Facebook, Instagram, YouTube, and Google Ads allow you to target specific demographics based on interests, behaviors, and viewing habits. A well-crafted ad campaign places your content in front of the right people, increasing brand awareness and driving more traffic to your show.

Sponsored posts on social media work well for showcasing trailers, teasers, or standout moments. With video-based ads, capturing attention within the first few seconds is crucial, so compelling hooks—such as dramatic soundbites or bold visuals—ensure better engagement. Running ads encouraging viewers to follow, subscribe, or engage with your content directly can also lead to long-term audience retention.

Influencer partnerships can act as another form of paid promotion. Rather than traditional ads, working with established creators to feature your show or mention it in their content provides credibility and introduces your work to a pre-built audience. This approach feels more natural than standard advertising and often leads to better viewer engagement.

Finding the Right Balance

Relying entirely on paid promotion can become expensive and unsustainable without a strong foundation of organic engagement. Paid ads might bring in initial clicks, but if the content doesn't keep viewers interested, those viewers won't stick around. Conversely, depending only on organic growth can limit exposure, making it difficult to break into competitive markets.

A balanced approach involves using paid ads for strategic boosts—such as promoting a season launch or a major guest appearance—while maintaining organic engagement for steady, lasting growth. Focusing on high-quality content, active community-building, and smart advertising creates a cycle where new viewers discover your show, engage with it, and then naturally spread it further. This synergy ensures that short-term visibility and long-term audience loyalty continue growing.

CHAPTER 12

Monetization Strategies

Turning a show into a source of income requires careful planning and the right monetization strategies. While creativity and audience engagement remain at the heart of any successful program, financial sustainability ensures that content production can continue and improve over time. From direct viewer support to brand partnerships and ad revenue, multiple ways exist to generate income without compromising the show's integrity. By selecting the right mix of monetization methods, creators can balance profitability and maintaining a strong, engaged audience.

Sponsorship and Ad Placements

Sponsorships and ad placements are among the most effective ways to monetize a show, offering financial support while expanding brand visibility. However, finding the right partners requires more than just securing a deal—ensuring alignment between the brand's message and your show's tone, values, and audience expectations. A well-matched sponsorship enhances credibility and feels natural, while a poorly chosen partnership can alienate viewers and weaken trust. Striking the right balance allows you to generate revenue while maintaining the integrity of your content.

Identifying the Right Brand Partners

The first step in securing sponsorships is identifying companies or brands that align with your show's theme and audience demographics. A tech-focused program may seek partnerships with gadget manufacturers, software companies, or online learning platforms. A health and wellness show would be better suited for fitness brands, organic food companies, or meditation apps. The key is to find sponsors whose products or services naturally fit within the topics you cover so promotions feel like a valuable addition rather than a forced interruption.

Understanding your audience is crucial. Brands want to work with shows that reach their ideal customers, so knowing viewer demographics—such as age range, interests, and spending habits—makes your pitch stronger. Gathering data from social media insights, viewer comments, or surveys can help demonstrate your audience's buying potential. The more clearly you can define your viewer base, the more attractive you become to sponsors looking for targeted exposure.

Types of Sponsorship and Ad Placements

There are several ways to integrate sponsored content into your show without making it feel intrusive. One of the most effective methods is **native sponsorship**, where the brand is seamlessly woven into the content. This might involve discussing a product that naturally fits into the episode's topic or demonstrating how it works in a way that feels organic. For example, if your show focuses on productivity, showcasing a sponsor's time-management app as part of an episode about improving efficiency makes the ad feel relevant and useful rather than disruptive.

Pre-roll and mid-roll ads are another common approach. These short, dedicated sponsor messages appear before or during the show. While these ads are more structured than native sponsorships, they can still be engaging if presented creatively. Rather than simply reading a generic script, adding personal insights or humor can make these segments feel more like a recommendation than a commercial.

Another form of monetization is **affiliate partnerships**, where you earn commissions for sales made through your referrals. Some sponsors provide personalized discount codes or affiliate links, incentivizing viewers to purchase while supporting your show. This method works best when you genuinely believe in the product, as viewers are likelier to act on sincere recommendations.

Maintaining Authenticity and Audience Trust

Regardless of how sponsorships are incorporated, maintaining authenticity is key. Viewers quickly recognize when a host promotes something just for the paycheck rather than genuine interest. Transparency is essential—disclose sponsorships and partnerships so the audience knows when content is being monetized. Most platforms and industry guidelines require disclosure, but beyond compliance, honesty fosters trust. A simple acknowledgment like, "This episode is sponsored by [Brand], a product I use and recommend," reassures viewers that you're upfront about the relationship.

Being selective with sponsorships strengthens credibility. Turning down deals that don't align with your values or audience expectations may mean fewer short-term earnings, but it preserves long-term viewer loyalty. A sponsorship that feels forced or off-brand risks damaging your reputation and driving viewers away.

Sponsorships and ad placements provide a reliable source of income when done thoughtfully. By choosing brands that align with your content, naturally integrating promotions, and maintaining transparency with your audience, you can create a monetization strategy that benefits your show and viewers. When handled well, sponsorships don't just generate revenue—they enhance the overall experience, adding value to your content while keeping your audience engaged and supportive.

Subscription Models and Memberships

A subscription or membership program can transform passive viewers into dedicated supporters while providing a stable income. Instead of relying solely on ads or sponsorships, this approach allows your audience to contribute directly, ensuring long-term sustainability. The key to success lies in offering meaningful perks that make subscribers feel valued while keeping the free content engaging enough to attract new viewers.

To encourage people to join, you must offer something they can't get elsewhere. Exclusive content is one of the biggest draws. This could include extended interviews, behind-the-scenes footage, or early access to episodes. Subscribers appreciate feeling like insiders, so offering content that gives them a deeper look into your creative process or access to unaired material makes the membership feel special. Some creators provide members-only discussions, sharing personal insights or industry secrets unavailable in the regular show.

Another popular incentive is direct interaction. Fans who support your content often want to feel a personal connection, and memberships can provide that opportunity. Hosting live Q&A sessions, giving personalized shoutouts, or allowing members to vote on upcoming topics fosters a sense of involvement. Some shows even create private online groups where members can interact with each other and the host, strengthening the community. When viewers feel their contributions shape the content, they become more invested in the show's success.

Choosing the right platform for managing subscriptions is important. Many creators use services like Patreon, YouTube Channel Memberships, or Buy Me a Coffee, each offering different ways to provide exclusive perks. Some platforms take a percentage of earnings, while others give full control over pricing and benefits. Integrating a direct membership option allows complete ownership of your audience and revenue if you have a website. Understanding the best fit for your content ensures a smoother experience for you and your subscribers.

Finding the right balance between free and paid content is essential. Offering too much for free can reduce the incentive to subscribe, but locking everything behind a paywall can limit audience growth. A good approach is to keep your main episodes accessible to everyone while reserving extras like bonus content or ad-free versions for paying members. A free trial or limited-time discount can also encourage people to test the benefits before committing.

Sustaining a membership program requires ongoing effort. If perks remain static, people may lose interest and cancel. Keeping subscribers engaged means consistently adding value through fresh content, interactive events, or member-only updates. Checking in with members and asking what they want to see can help refine the offerings.

Beyond financial benefits, a membership model strengthens the bond between you and your audience. Supporters aren't just paying for extra content; they're investing in the continued success of something they enjoy. A well-structured program fosters loyalty, turning casual viewers into long-term fans who actively contribute to the show's growth.

Diversifying Revenue Streams

Relying on a single source of income can be risky, especially in the fast-changing digital landscape. Diversifying revenue streams ensures financial stability while offering multiple ways for viewers to support your show. Expanding into areas like merchandise, affiliate marketing, and crowdfunding allows for steady earnings without over-relying on advertising or sponsorships. Each method provides unique advantages, catering to different audience preferences and levels of commitment.

Merchandise as a Branding Tool

Selling branded products is an effective way to generate income while strengthening audience loyalty. Merchandise turns casual viewers into ambassadors, as wearing or using show-related items spreads awareness. The key to successful March sales is offering items that genuinely resonate with your audience. Clothing, mugs, posters, or stickers featuring popular catchphrases, inside jokes, or unique artwork related to your content perform well. Limited-edition drops or seasonal designs create urgency, encouraging fans to purchase while supplies last.

Setting up an online store has become easier with platforms like Shopify, Tee Spring, or Printful, which handle production and shipping. This allows creators to focus on design and promotion rather than logistics. Additionally, integrating store links into social media pages and streaming platforms increases visibility and makes purchasing more convenient for fans.

Affiliate Marketing for Passive Income

Affiliate marketing allows you to earn commissions by recommending products or services relevant to your audience. This is particularly effective if your content involves product discussions, reviews, or tutorials. Rather than relying on random sponsorships, affiliate partnerships give you control over what you promote, ensuring alignment with your brand and values.

Many companies offer affiliate programs, providing unique tracking links or discount codes. Every time a viewer purchases through your link, you receive a percentage of the sale. Amazon Associates, Share A Sale, and individual brand partnerships are common ways to start. The key is promoting genuinely useful products, as authenticity builds trust. Viewers are more likely to follow recommendations when they receive honest, valuable insights rather than a forced sales pitch.

Crowdfunding for Community Support

Crowdfunding provides direct audience support for creators who want to remain independent without relying heavily on ads or sponsorships. Platforms like Patreon, Kickstarter, and Ko-fi allow fans to contribute financially in exchange for perks like exclusive content, behind-the-scenes access, or personal interactions. Unlike one-time purchases, crowdfunding often involves recurring contributions, making it a reliable revenue stream.

The success of a crowdfunding campaign depends on how well it connects with supporters. Meaningful incentives encourage contributions, whether early access to episodes, custom shootouts, or limited-edition merchandise. Transparency also plays a big role—letting backers know how their funds are used fosters trust and encourages long-term support.

Building a Sustainable Income

A well-rounded approach to monetization blends multiple income sources, allowing flexibility and financial security. Merchandise appeals to fans who want a tangible connection to the show, affiliate marketing provides passive income through trusted recommendations, and crowdfunding creates a strong community-driven financial base. By integrating these methods thoughtfully, creators can ensure their content remains profitable while maintaining a positive relationship with their audience.

The key to success in any revenue strategy is staying authentic. When monetization feels natural and aligns with the content, viewers are more willing to support it. You can build a sustainable income model that keeps your show and its community thriving by continuously refining your approach and listening to audience feedback.

CHAPTER 13

As a show grows, so do its demands. Managing everything alone can become overwhelming, making it necessary to expand operations and bring in a team. Scaling up involves refining workflows, improving production quality, and delegating tasks to ensure smoother execution. Whether hiring editors, producers, social media managers, or marketing specialists, building the right team allows for greater efficiency and creative growth. A well-structured team lightens the workload and brings fresh perspectives, helping the show evolve while maintaining consistency.

When to Expand Your Team

Expanding a team is crucial in taking a show to the next level, but the timing must be right. Hiring too soon can lead to unnecessary costs while waiting too long can result in burnout and missed growth opportunities. The decision to bring in additional help should come when tasks become overwhelming, content quality starts slipping, or the workload prevents you from focusing on creative development. Recognizing when and who to hire can make all the difference in maintaining consistency and scaling effectively.

One of the clearest signs that it's time to expand is when production schedules become difficult to maintain. If deadlines are constantly pushed back or episodes feel rushed, the workload may have grown beyond what one person can handle. A growing audience brings higher expectations, and ensuring content remains polished and engaging requires sufficient time and effort. If managing research, scripting, filming, editing, and promotion alone feels unsustainable, bringing in support can restore balance and improve overall production quality.

Another indicator is when administrative and technical tasks begin to overshadow creative work. Producing a show involves more than just recording and editing—scheduling, marketing, audience interaction, and sponsorship management. If too much time is spent on logistics rather than refining content, hiring a producer or assistant can help streamline operations. Delegating tasks like social media updates, coordinating with guests, or handling sponsorship negotiations allows more energy to be dedicated to crafting engaging episodes.

Audience engagement is another area where additional help can be beneficial. As a show gains traction, keeping up with viewer comments, emails, and messages becomes more time-consuming. Interaction is essential for building loyalty, but it cannot be easy to manage alongside content creation. Bringing in a social media manager or community coordinator ensures that viewers remain engaged and valued, strengthening the show's connection with its audience.

When selecting the first team members, it's important to prioritize roles that directly address the biggest challenges. If editing takes too long, hiring an editor allows for a faster turnaround while maintaining quality. If researching and scripting are overwhelming, bringing in a researcher or content assistant can improve the depth and structure of episodes. The goal is to relieve pressure in areas that most slow down production, making the overall workflow more efficient.

Building a team isn't just about hiring people but creating a shared vision. Whether adding a producer, researcher, editor, or co-host, each person should complement the show's direction and bring value to its growth. Clear communication, well-defined roles, and a collaborative mindset help ensure that expansion strengthens the project rather than complicating it.

Knowing when to expand and selecting the right team members is a balancing act. Still, when done strategically, it leads to better content, a more engaged audience, and a smoother production process. Growth is an ongoing journey, and surrounding yourself with the right support makes it easier to sustain and evolve the show while staying true to its core vision.

Delegating Responsibilities

As a show grows, managing every aspect alone becomes impractical. While handling everything from scripting to editing to promotion may work in the early stages, the increasing demands of a larger audience and more complex production eventually require delegation. Learning to distribute responsibilities effectively allows you to focus on on-camera work while ensuring that technical and administrative tasks are handled efficiently. This shift improves content quality and prevents burnout, making the production process more sustainable in the long run.

The first step in delegation is identifying which tasks take the most time and which can be handled by someone else without compromising creative control. Technical aspects like video editing, sound mixing, and graphic design often fall into this category. These elements are crucial for maintaining a professional look but don't necessarily require the host's direct involvement. Hiring an experienced editor can enhance visual and audio quality while freeing scripting, interviews, or performance preparation time.

Administrative work is another area where delegation can make a big difference. Tasks such as scheduling guests, responding to emails, managing sponsorship agreements, and updating social media platforms can consume hours that could be better-spent refining content. Bringing in a producer or virtual assistant to handle these responsibilities allows for a smoother workflow and ensures that nothing important gets overlooked. A well-organized team can manage communication, coordinate logistics, and maintain consistency without distracting the creative process.

Marketing and audience engagement also benefit from delegation. Social media managers or community coordinators can monitor comments, engage with viewers, and analyze audience insights to refine content strategy. While personal interaction remains important, especially for building relationships with fans, having dedicated support ensures a more active and responsive presence across platforms. Regular engagement helps retain viewers and attract new ones, strengthening the show's long-term impact.

Trust is essential when handing off responsibilities. Micromanaging every detail defeats, the purpose of delegation and can slow down progress. Selecting team members who understand the show's vision and have the necessary skills allows tasks to be completed with minimal supervision. Setting clear expectations, providing constructive feedback, and maintaining open communication help build a team that operates smoothly. Checking in regularly ensures that everything stays aligned with the show's standards without requiring constant oversight.

The transition from working solo to leading a team can be challenging but opens up new creative possibilities. With technical and administrative tasks handled efficiently, more energy can be devoted to improving performance, developing engaging content, and exploring new ideas. A reliable support system makes experimenting with different formats, expanding production quality, or introducing fresh elements that enhance the viewer experience easier.

Delegating is not about stepping away from responsibilities but optimizing the most available resources. By shifting focus to on-camera work while allowing a capable team to manage the behind-the-scenes elements, the overall quality and consistency of the show improve. This approach leads to better content, a stronger audience connection, and a more sustainable production process, ensuring long-term success.

Enhancing production quality transforms a show from basic to professional, creating a more immersive experience for viewers. While compelling content draws people in, clear visuals, crisp sound, and an appealing set keep them engaged. Upgrading equipment, refining editing techniques, and improving the studio environment contribute to a polished final product. These investments elevate the viewing experience and help build credibility and audience loyalty.

A sharp, well-lit image makes a strong impression. Many creators start with built-in webcams or smartphone cameras, but upgrading to a DSLR or mirrorless model provides better color accuracy and depth. Proper lighting is just as important as camera quality. Softbox lights, LED panels, or ring lights enhance clarity by eliminating harsh shadows and improving skin tones. Simple adjustments, like strategically positioning a desk lamp or using natural light effectively, can make a difference.

Sound quality plays a major role in keeping audiences engaged. Viewers may tolerate minor video issues, but poor audio can quickly turn them away. Built-in microphones often pick up background noise, making speech unclear. Investing in an external microphone, whether a USB model for easy setup or an XLR version for professional-grade sound, significantly improves clarity. Positioning the microphone correctly and using accessories like pop filters or windscreens enhances vocal crispness.

Editing software refines raw footage into a seamless final product. Professional tools like Adobe Premiere Pro, Final Cut Pro, or DaVinci Resolve allow precise adjustments to color, transitions, and effects. Streaming software such as OBS Studio or vMix for live broadcasts ensures smooth scene changes, overlays, and real-time graphics. Advanced audio software helps remove background noise and balance sound levels, ensuring consistent episode quality.

The studio environment also impacts production value. A well-organized set makes the presentation visually appealing while reinforcing the show's identity. Backgrounds should be clean and uncluttered, avoiding distractions. Simple improvements, like using a solid-color backdrop, adding soft accent lighting, or placing relevant props, create a polished aesthetic. Small details, such as matching the color scheme to the show's branding, add a cohesive touch without requiring a major budget.

Improving production quality doesn't mean spending excessively all at once. Gradual upgrades immediately impact immediately, starting with the most noticeable elements like lighting and audio. Over time, refining visuals, optimizing the workspace, and incorporating better technology lead to a more engaging experience. A high-quality production attracts new viewers and keeps them coming back, helping the show grow and establish a professional reputation.

CHAPTER 14

Overcoming Hurdles and Challenges

Every show, no matter how well-planned, faces challenges along the way. Technical difficulties, creative blocks, audience fluctuations, and unexpected setbacks are all part of the journey. Success isn't about avoiding these hurdles but learning how to navigate them effectively. By staying adaptable, problem-solving efficiently, and maintaining a clear vision, it's possible to turn obstacles into opportunities for growth. The ability to handle difficulties with confidence strengthens the show's quality and builds resilience, ensuring long-term success in an ever-changing industry.

Technical Glitches and On-Air Mishaps

Technical issues are unavoidable when hosting a show, no matter how well-prepared you are. Sound failures, buffering, and unexpected interruptions can disrupt the flow, but how you handle them makes all the difference. Staying calm, diagnosing the problem quickly, and having a plan in place can turn a potential disaster into a minor inconvenience. The key is preparation, adaptability, and connecting with your audience while resolving the issue.

One of the most common challenges is sound failure. A microphone may suddenly stop working, audio could become distorted, or background noise might interfere with clarity. The first step is to check the basics—ensuring the microphone is properly connected, the right input source is selected, and volume levels are balanced. Sometimes, a simple loose cable or an accidental mute button press is the cause. A backup microphone can save valuable time if the primary one fails. Testing equipment before going live and using headphones to monitor real-time audio helps detect issues early, preventing major disruptions.

Internet connection problems can cause buffering, lag, or dropped streams, frustrating both the host and viewers. A slow or unstable connection often leads to choppy video and audio, making it difficult for the audience to follow the conversation. Testing internet speed before streaming ensures the connection is strong enough to handle live broadcasting. A wired Ethernet connection is generally more stable than Wi-Fi, reducing the risk of sudden drops. Switching to a lower streaming resolution or adjusting bitrate settings can improve stability if issues arise during a live session. Some broadcasting platforms allow automatic bitrate adjustments, ensuring smoother playback even when network conditions fluctuate.

Unexpected on-air disruptions are another challenge, whether it's a guest losing connection, a power outage, or background noise interfering with the show. Remaining composed reassures viewers and maintains professionalism. A quick acknowledgment of the issue, such as, "Looks like we're having a small technical issue—bear with us for a moment," keeps the audience engaged rather than leaving them confused. If a guest disconnects, transitioning smoothly to another topic or engaging with the audience through a quick Q&A session prevents awkward silence. Having a co-host or moderator can also help manage unexpected gaps, ensuring the show continues without a long pause.

Preventative measures go a long way in minimizing technical problems. Regularly checking all equipment, updating software, and rehearsing before going live reduces the likelihood of major disruptions. Testing microphones, cameras, and streaming software ensure everything functions correctly before the broadcast begins. Keeping extra cables, backup power sources, and alternative internet options available can prevent minor problems from turning into full-blown crises.

Even with the best preparation, technical issues will occasionally happen. What matters most is the ability to handle them with confidence and professionalism. When hosts remain calm and focused, viewers are likelier to stay engaged rather than tune out. Over time, troubleshooting becomes second nature, making it easier to adapt to unexpected situations without losing momentum. By prioritizing preparation and quick problem-solving, any technical mishap can be managed smoothly, keeping the show running without compromising quality.

Managing Negative Feedback and Trolls

Feedback is an unavoidable part of putting content out into the world. No matter how well a show is produced, there will always be opinions, suggestions, and, at times, outright hostility. Learning how to handle criticism while maintaining professionalism is crucial. Engaging positively with constructive feedback, setting clear community guidelines, and knowing when to ignore harmful negativity can make a significant difference in maintaining a supportive audience while protecting your mental well-being.

Not all criticism is bad. Some feedback comes from viewers who genuinely want to see improvements. A comment pointing out an unclear explanation, a pacing issue, or a technical flaw may seem negative initially but could provide valuable insights. Acknowledging these comments with gratitude and considering them for future episodes helps build a stronger connection with the audience. Responding with appreciation, such as, "That's a great point! I'll work on improving that," shows openness to growth without taking criticism personally.

At times, criticism may come across as harsh or unfair. A viewer might express frustration over a particular segment or strongly disagree with an opinion shared on the show. In such cases, staying calm is essential. Reacting defensively or arguing back only escalates tension. Instead, taking a step back and assessing whether there's any merit to the criticism can lead to a more constructive response. If a comment feels aggressive but still touches on an important issue, addressing it diplomatically can turn it into a positive interaction. For instance, responding with, "I understand your perspective, and I appreciate you sharing it," helps defuse hostility while keeping the conversation open.

Then, some trolls seek to provoke a reaction rather than provide meaningful feedback. These comments often contain insults, inflammatory statements, or completely unrelated negativity. Engaging with trolls is rarely productive, as they aim to get attention rather than participate in a real discussion. Ignoring them or using platform moderation tools to filter harmful comments is often the best approach. Many streaming platforms and social media sites offer features to block or restrict users who repeatedly disrupt discussions. Removing toxic influences from the comment section keeps the space welcoming for those who engage in good faith.

A strong community thrives on respect and open dialogue. Setting clear guidelines for interactions ensures that discussions remain productive. Outlining expectations in descriptions, chat rules, or pinned messages lets viewers know what behavior is acceptable. Prohibiting hate speech, personal attacks, and spam while allowing honest feedback helps strike the right balance. If a viewer crosses the line, issuing a polite but firm warning or enforcing timeouts can prevent further disruptions.

How a host responds to criticism shapes the overall tone of the community? If negative comments are met with hostility, the audience may adopt a similar attitude, leading to a toxic environment. On the other hand, maintaining a level-headed and professional demeanor encourages respectful discussions. Over time, viewers will follow the example set by the show's creator, leading to a healthier, more engaged audience.

Dealing with feedback requires patience and emotional control. Some criticism will be useful, some will be unnecessary, and some will be meant purely to provoke. The key is learning to separate helpful input from harmful negativity while fostering a space where discussions can occur without hostility. By maintaining composure and setting clear boundaries, content creators can protect their work and well-being, ensuring that their show continues to grow in a positive and supportive environment.

Staying Motivated and Avoiding Burnout

Creating and hosting a show requires dedication, creativity, and consistent effort. While passion drives the process, the demands of planning, recording, editing, and engaging with an audience can become overwhelming over time. Without proper balance, burnout can creep in, affecting both the quality of content and personal well-being. Staying motivated requires setting realistic goals, managing work-life balance, and recognizing achievements.

One of the biggest challenges in content creation is maintaining enthusiasm over the long term. In the early stages, excitement fuels creativity, but the pressure to constantly produce can feel exhausting as the workload increases. Setting clear, achievable goals helps maintain focus and prevents frustration. Instead of aiming for perfection in every episode, breaking down tasks into smaller steps makes the process more manageable. Planning content in advance, maintaining a schedule that allows for flexibility, and setting realistic deadlines prevent unnecessary stress while ensuring steady progress.

Work-life balance is essential to staying energized and avoiding creative fatigue. Spending too much time on production, research, and promotion can lead to exhaustion, making it harder to stay inspired. Scheduling regular breaks, setting boundaries between work and personal life, and prioritizing rest help maintain long-term productivity. Engaging in hobbies, exercising, or spending time with family and friends creates a necessary mental reset, preventing burnout and keeping creativity flowing.

Burnout often stems from over-commitment. Trying to handle every aspect of production alone can become overwhelming. Delegating tasks, whether by hiring help or using automation tools, reduces pressure and allows for greater focus on the most important aspects of the show. Bringing in editors, social media managers, or research assistants lightens the load, making the process more sustainable. A well-balanced workflow leads to better results and a more enjoyable creative experience.

Finding motivation in small victories can make a big difference. Celebrating milestones, such as reaching a subscriber goal, completing a difficult episode, or receiving positive feedback, reinforces progress. Acknowledging these achievements helps shift focus from the pressures of growth to the fulfillment of creating meaningful content. Recognizing audience engagement—whether through comments, shares, or messages of appreciation—also serves as a reminder of why the show was started in the first place.

Staying inspired requires continuous learning and adaptation. Exploring new topics, experimenting with different formats, or collaborating with other creators brings fresh energy to the show. Taking breaks to watch other content, read, or attend industry events introduces new ideas and perspectives, preventing creative stagnation. Keeping an open mind and allowing room for innovation ensures the creative process remains exciting rather than repetitive.

Avoiding burnout doesn't mean avoiding hard work; it means working smarter. Balancing effort with rest, setting attainable goals, and celebrating progress contribute to a sustainable and fulfilling content creation journey. Passion remains at the heart of every great show but requires care and self-awareness. With the right approach, motivation stays strong, and the creative process thrives without feeling like a burden.

CHAPTER 15

How to distribute a show can feel like a defining moment for creators. Some prefer the independence of launching on personal platforms or through open streaming services, enjoying full control over branding and content decisions. Others embrace the backing of established networks, gaining access to bigger budgets, large built-in audiences, and marketing support. Neither path guarantees success or avoids challenges; it all depends on priorities, goals, and comfort with risk. By weighing creative freedom against the resources a network provides, creators can make a decision that best aligns with their show's unique vision.

Evaluating Your Resources and Goals

Determining how to bring a show to the public can be an exhilarating challenge. Creators often wonder if it's better to self-finance and maintain full creative control or to join forces with a network for broader exposure. Each option has advantages and potential pitfalls, and the right choice depends on budget, artistic vision, and long-term ambitions. Below is a closer look at how to weigh these factors, along with some guiding bullet points to help clarify the thought process.

Budget and Creative Control

Self-Funding Benefits

Financing the show independently can preserve your vision, since there's no need to accommodate external demands. Creators with strong niche audiences or clear branding can often tap into crowdfunding, sponsorships, or personal savings to support a season's production. This route enables full ownership of the final product, letting you experiment with unconventional story arcs, filming techniques, or release schedules without external constraints.

Network Partnerships

Working with a network can significantly expand the budget available for filming locations, special effects, top-tier equipment, and even star talent. Networks also tend to have established marketing and PR teams, which may reduce the time you need to spend on promotion. However, their investment typically comes with a say in creative decisions. Producers might request changes to scripts, casting, or episode runtimes to fit existing brand identities or audience expectations. Overriding network feedback can be an uphill battle, especially if they're covering most or all of the costs.

Finding Balance

Some creators split funding between personal resources and partial network deals, maintaining a measure of independence while benefiting from a portion of the network's infrastructure. Others negotiate terms that limit a network's creative influence, though this often means accepting a smaller budget or less promotional support. The trick is to protect what makes the show unique while ensuring you have enough funding to execute that vision effectively.

Risk vs. Reward

Going Solo

If your show's identity aligns closely with an existing community—such as a niche fandom or professional group—self-launching can build deeper connections and loyalty. Retaining full creative direction can be a major selling point, especially if the audience values authenticity above all else. However, going solo also means bearing financial losses if production costs outweigh revenue, and dealing with all the logistical tasks, from editing and distribution to marketing. It's a high-reward scenario if everything clicks, but it requires considerable planning and resourcefulness to avoid burnout or budget shortfalls.

Partnering with a Network

Network backing can speed up growth, giving your show access to large, built-in audiences and the credibility that comes from association with a recognized brand. Strong marketing pushes and potential cross-promotion with existing shows can accelerate momentum. The downside is that your brand identity might be overshadowed or reshaped by the network's internal directives. Creators who thrive under structure—willing to adapt plotlines or formats—can benefit immensely, whereas those with strictly defined visions may struggle. Although working with a network can be safer financially, the trade-off usually involves surrendering a degree of creative autonomy.

Aligning with Personal Goals

Choosing whether to go it alone or team up with a network is ultimately about knowing what kind of creator you are. If the main objective is complete authorship, independence makes sense; if you aim for rapid scaling and broad-based appeal, a network's resources might be indispensable. Some creators begin independently, then transition to networks after proving their concept, striking better deals because they already have momentum. Others find that a network's constraints stifle the raw energy that drew fans in the first place.

Assessing budget requirements and gauging how much control you're willing to trade for financial and promotional advantages are central to deciding whether solo distribution or a network partnership is right for you. There's no one-size-fits-all model. Each approach has success stories—from indie darlings that break through on personal platforms to network-backed hits that draw millions of viewers. Reflecting on the show's essence, audience expectations, and your tolerance for creative risk can guide a thoughtful decision that aligns with both immediate needs and long-term aspirations.

Negotiating with Potential Networks

Entering discussions with a potential network can be both exciting and intimidating. On one hand, a network partnership may unlock larger budgets, wider reach, and seasoned production support. On the other hand, giving up a portion of creative control and navigating complex contracts can pose serious challenges. A well-prepared approach—grounded in research, realistic expectations, and clear communication—helps ensure that both you and the network find common ground.

Finding the right fit often begins with understanding each network's brand, programming style, and audience demographics. A network known for high-energy reality shows may not be the best match for a contemplative docuseries, while a distributor with a track record in animated content could be the perfect fit for your latest cartoon venture. Identifying platforms that already draw viewers similar to those you hope to reach is a smart tactic. It often means less competition for attention within the network's lineup and a greater chance that existing subscribers will try your show. Examining production quality, marketing strategies, and how the network interacts with its talent also provides insight into day-to-day realities of working together. Creators often find it helpful to speak with peers who have launched shows on the platform, gaining unfiltered perspectives on the network's efficiency, reliability, and communication style.

When network representatives express interest, it's crucial to be well-versed in standard contract terms. Common elements include revenue splits, licensing agreements, and distribution rights. Some contracts offer a flat fee in exchange for exclusive rights, while others structure payments around performance milestones—such as view counts or subscription increases attributed to your show. Balancing a fair split of revenue with the desire to retain creative freedom can be tricky, especially if the network is providing substantial funding. You might negotiate for production or marketing support in return for a slightly higher percentage of earnings going to the network, as long as it doesn't compromise your show's fundamental identity.

Beyond finances, licensing and ownership terms heavily influence long-term possibilities. When a network obtains full ownership of your show's intellectual property, it can gain the power to make sequels, spin-offs, or adaptations without your involvement. If you hope to expand the show's universe through merchandise or international streaming partnerships, ensure the contract clarifies who has the final say in these decisions. Some creators prefer a co-ownership model, or at least carve out certain rights—like the freedom to create derivative works—so that they retain partial creative control. Negotiating favorable terms usually requires a willingness to push back on overreaching clauses and, in many cases, consultation with an entertainment attorney.

Safeguarding creative vision throughout negotiations is about more than just contract language. Setting boundaries, such as maintaining final approval on key creative decisions—storylines, casting, or stylistic elements—helps preserve the show's authenticity. You may need to compromise on certain issues, such as episode length or release schedules, if the network's model demands adjustments. However, clarifying must-have aspects early on ensures that these elements remain protected. Open communication goes a long way: demonstrating both flexibility and steadfastness in areas that define your show can establish mutual respect.

Negotiating with a network involves not just hammering out a deal but also assessing whether the partnership supports the show's future. If the network's track record, contract provisions, or creative preferences seem incompatible, it may be best to walk away, even if the offer appears financially tempting. When the right match comes along, a well-constructed agreement can amplify your show's reach and creative ambitions, setting the stage for lasting success.

CHAPTER 16

Exploring Various Streaming Platforms and Networks

Choosing the right streaming platforms or networks can determine whether your show stands out or fades away. Each service comes with its own audience, programming style, and content preferences, so it's crucial to find one that aligns with your show's identity. By understanding these differences, you can pick the best fit, reach the right viewers, and give your production the attention it deserves.

Global Entertainment Platforms

Over-the-top (OTT) platforms have reshaped the entertainment landscape, allowing creators to distribute shows directly to global audiences without traditional broadcast constraints. Major names like Netflix, Hulu, and Amazon Prime Video carry the weight of vast subscriber bases and deep pockets for original content. Alongside these giants, newer or more niche services—Tubi among them—have carved out their own space, appealing to viewers seeking specific types of shows, particular genres, or a budget-friendly viewing experience. Deciding which of these platforms might host a series depends on a range of factors, from the show's target demographic to the creator's long-term aspirations.

For those aiming to capture the widest possible audience, signing with a heavyweight like Netflix can offer immense visibility, often making a show a household name overnight. Netflix subscribers tune in from around the globe, which can spark organic word-of-mouth in regions a creator may not have anticipated. Additionally, Netflix is known for investing in original productions that span myriad genres: reality competitions, cutting-edge animation, stand-up specials, and prestige dramas among them. For a show that fits the platform's broad appeal—and that has the potential to stand up against the service's extensive library—this partnership might lead to a surge in followers and critical attention. However, Netflix's rigorous selection process and constant influx of fresh titles also create intense competition. Any show listed must stand out quickly to avoid being buried beneath newer releases.

While Netflix can be a goldmine for creators who secure a deal, smaller shows sometimes benefit more from services geared toward specific demographics. Tubi is an example of a free ad-supported platform that many viewers turn to for budget-friendly streaming. The cost-free access draws an audience open to lesser-known or specialized content, which can serve as an ideal environment for shows that might be too niche for larger outlets or lack the budget for a massive licensing fee. Here, being a big fish in a smaller pond can boost visibility, as viewers interested in a particular style or theme may find the show organically through curated categories. At the same time, creators must be prepared for ad breaks and a different revenue model, one that relies on advertising rather than subscription fees. While this structure can feel less lucrative, it can also make the show more accessible to those unwilling or unable to pay for premium subscriptions.

Niche discovery can be powerful. Whether through Tubi, Shudder (for horror enthusiasts), or BritBox (for British television), certain platforms gravitate toward curated selections, ensuring viewers come back for more in that specialized realm. Shows anchored in a distinct genre—science fiction, classic anime, vintage sitcoms—may thrive when offered alongside comparable titles, capturing a loyal following that actively searches for content in that category. This type of audience may be smaller overall than those on major platforms, but they're often more engaged, translating to higher completion rates and word-of-mouth recommendations. Niche platforms also occasionally offer flexible licensing terms and promotional boosts for original or exclusive titles that align with their brand identity.

Creators thus find themselves weighing visibility against audience specificity. Where Netflix might deliver millions of potential eyeballs, Tubi and other specialized platforms can provide an environment where competition for attention is less fierce. For a show with a clear market segment or limited promotional budget, seeking out a service that caters to a particular taste can lead to a solid core audience, even if the overall numbers are smaller than what a massive service can deliver. The key is aligning the show's content—theme, style, and ambitions—with the ethos and user base of the chosen platform, ensuring that the people who would appreciate it the most are the ones most likely to see it.

Professional and Business-Focused Channels

Professional and business-focused channels offer a more targeted approach to content distribution, serving viewers who value expert insights, thought leadership, and industry-specific topics. Rather than appealing to broad, mainstream entertainment audiences, these platforms concentrate on elevating serious discussions, specialized knowledge, or empowerment narratives that align with specific professional or cultural segments. For creators whose shows revolve around topics such as entrepreneurship, women's leadership, or innovative technology, working with networks like World Broadcast Network TV or Women's Broadcast Network can be a strategic move toward finding highly engaged audiences.

World Broadcast Network TV focuses on reaching business professionals, industry insiders, and subject-matter experts. These viewers often have more specialized viewing habits, actively seeking educational or informative programming that helps them stay up-to-date in their fields. The network's emphasis on B2B content positions it as a platform where shows featuring interviews with CEOs, roundtable discussions on market trends, or instructional series on professional development can flourish. For creators, the advantage lies in tapping into a base of viewers who are already motivated to watch material relevant to their careers. A program dissecting global finance or offering advice on effective leadership styles might draw a more loyal following here than on a mainstream service that caters to diverse tastes. Additionally, business-focused platforms often provide opportunities for cross-promotion, such as sponsored webinars or live panels, enhancing the show's visibility within specific professional spheres.

Closely related to this concept of specialized networks is the Women's Broadcast Network, which speaks directly to female audiences looking for content shaped by or spotlighting women's perspectives. In recent years, there has been a growing appetite for storytelling that challenges traditional roles and celebrates women's achievements across all areas of life—from business and politics to family and creative endeavors. The Women's Broadcast Network capitalizes on this demand by curating shows that put female-driven narratives at the forefront. Creators featuring stories of women-led startups, mother-daughter relationships, or innovative personal journeys may find a receptive audience ready to champion their success. Aligning with this platform can also signal a commitment to diversity and representation, potentially attracting viewers who seek inspirational, empowering media.

Working with these networks brings certain benefits beyond a narrower but committed viewership. Advertisers and sponsors on specialized channels are often more focused themselves, catering to audiences with more defined purchasing or professional habits. That can translate to more lucrative sponsorship deals if a show's content aligns with these marketers' goals. At the same time, creators should be prepared to maintain higher levels of quality and credibility. Business professionals and those engaged in female empowerment narratives usually expect well-researched material, compelling storytelling, and clear value propositions, whether it's learning something new or feeling a personal connection to the topic.

Another advantage is the potential for networking within the platforms themselves. Producers, hosts, and thought leaders featured on these channels sometimes collaborate on cross-promotional efforts—joint episodes, panel discussions, or live events that bring together related shows under one virtual roof. Such cooperative efforts can expand a show's reach while reinforcing its reputation among an audience already inclined to seek out specialized programming.

Finding a home on a business-focused network or a channel dedicated to women's narratives requires a show to clearly communicate its purpose and appeal. When a production aligns well with a network's specific ethos, the collaboration can be especially rewarding: it pairs the right content with the right audience, fostering a sense of community that supports not just viewership but also ongoing conversation and influence in the real world.

Choosing the Right Platform

Selecting a suitable streaming platform is a decision that can profoundly influence your show's trajectory. With more distribution channels than ever, from mainstream giants to smaller niche networks, matching the show's content with the platform's audience and goals is key. Achieving this alignment comes down to two primary considerations: the demographics and interests of potential viewers, and whether the creator aims for broad exposure or prefers a focused but dedicated fanbase.

Understanding user demographics and interests is the first step. Each platform draws a specific group, influenced by programming styles, marketing, and brand identity. A show aimed at teens or young adults might find its best fit on social media–integrated services that specialize in short, dynamic content. Adult drama fans may respond more positively to premium services known for high-caliber series, such as HBO Max or Amazon Prime Video. In contrast, an educational talk show targeting business professionals might be better placed on networks that cater to a professional audience, where viewers are used to tuning in for informational or career-focused content. By studying the success stories and user reviews on a given platform, creators can glean whether their show's themes—be it sci-fi, cooking, or deep investigative reporting—will resonate with that service's subscriber base.

Researching how a platform handles promotion and discovery tools is equally important. Some platforms invest heavily in recommending new releases to users, boosting smaller projects alongside high-profile originals. Others concentrate most of their marketing resources on big-budget productions, leaving lesser-known shows with fewer promotional opportunities. Creators should weigh whether they're prepared to market on their own if the platform's promotional support is limited. If the show is directed at a niche crowd—such as fans of foreign-language arthouse films—picking a smaller platform that proudly highlights unique or specialty content could give it more immediate visibility than a massive service where it risks getting overlooked.

Long-term growth versus quick exposure is the second major factor in platform choice. Large, mainstream networks offer the chance to go viral quickly if a show captures audiences. Suddenly appearing on the service's main page or trending list can lead to a spike in viewership overnight. However, it can also result in a fleeting hype cycle, especially when users move on to the next big release. Other shows, particularly those built around a cult or niche appeal, can benefit from gradually growing a solid core audience on a smaller platform known for catering to devoted fans of that genre. In these cases, rather than massive, immediate numbers, creators focus on strengthening loyalty and encouraging word-of-mouth among a specialized community.

Finding that balance between breadth and depth depends on a show's inherent nature and the creator's objectives. If the goal is global acclaim, partnering with a mainstream service that routinely reaches millions may be the better bet. For productions with less universal appeal, focusing on a dedicated audience can foster passionate support, ultimately leading to a steadier, more sustainable model. This strategy may mean fewer viewers at first, but those who do tune in are generally enthusiastic, leaving positive reviews and advocating for the show's quality.

Picking a streaming platform involves a clear-eyed look at who the show is for and how it's best discovered. Matching themes with the right viewers is as vital as ensuring the network's promotional push meets expectations. Whether it aims for broad popularity or cultivates a devoted niche, the right platform can elevate a show from an interesting concept to a success story, simply by placing it in front of the people most likely to connect with its content.

CHAPTER 17

Reaching success with a show is achievable, but maintaining it requires ongoing effort, adaptation, and a forward-thinking mindset. Audiences evolve, industry trends shift, and new challenges arise, making it essential to continuously refine content, engage with viewers, and explore fresh opportunities. Growth isn't just about increasing numbers—it's about maintaining quality, staying relevant, and ensuring long-term sustainability. By embracing change, seeking innovation, and planning for the future, a show can thrive while remaining true to its core vision.

Evaluating Performance

Evaluating a show's performance is essential for long-term success. Simply producing content isn't enough—understanding how it resonates with the audience, which aspects work well, and where improvements can be made ensures steady growth. By analyzing viewership data, conversion rates, and audience engagement, creators can refine their approach, maximize impact, and maintain relevance in an ever-changing digital landscape.

Viewership data is one of the most telling indicators of a show's success. Tracking the number of views per episode provides insight into audience interest. A steady increase suggests growing popularity while fluctuating numbers might indicate engagement shifts or promotional strategies' effectiveness. However, total views alone don't tell the full story. Watch time and audience retention rates reveal how long viewers stay engaged. If most people drop off within the first few minutes, it may signal issues with pacing, content delivery, or an unengaging introduction. Adjusting format, improving storytelling, or refining episode structure can help maintain attention and increase viewer retention.

Conversion rates are another crucial metric, especially for monetization and audience interaction. Whether the goal is to drive subscriptions, encourage merchandise sales, or promote exclusive memberships, tracking how many viewers take action after watching an episode provides insight into effectiveness. If a call-to-action (CTA) at the end of a show leads to many sign-ups or sales, it's a sign that the message is resonating. If conversion rates are low, testing different approaches—such as clearer CTAs, limited-time offers, or incentives for engagement—can improve results.

Beyond numbers, audience engagement plays a key role in evaluating success. Comments, likes, shares, and social media discussions reflect how invested viewers are. A high level of interaction means the content sparks conversations and encourages community-building. Direct feedback from the audience, whether through polls, live chats, or Q&A sessions, provides valuable insights into what viewers enjoy and want to see more of. If engagement is low, making content more interactive, responding to comments, or incorporating viewer suggestions can help foster a stronger connection.

Comparing different episodes or seasons also highlights trends in performance. Noting which topics generate the most interest helps guide future content decisions. If certain types of episodes consistently outperform others, expanding on those themes can keep the show aligned with audience preferences. Experimenting with new formats while monitoring reactions allows innovation without straying too far from what works.

Data analysis should not replace creative instincts but complement them. While numbers provide a roadmap, balancing analytics with authentic storytelling ensures the show retains its unique voice. Adjustments based purely on data may lead to content that feels formulaic or disconnected, so it's important to interpret metrics while staying true to the show's vision.

A successful show evolves based on informed decisions rather than guesswork. Regularly evaluating viewership patterns, engagement levels, and conversion effectiveness allows continuous improvement. By understanding what resonates with the audience and making strategic adjustments, creators can sustain long-term success while keeping their content fresh and impactful.

Future-Proofing Your Show

Ensuring that a show remains relevant over time requires adapting to industry changes, new technologies, and shifts in audience behavior. The digital landscape evolves rapidly, with new platforms emerging, content consumption habits shifting, and technological advancements reshaping media production and distribution. Future-proofing a show means staying ahead of these changes, embracing innovation, and continuously refining the approach to maintain audience interest. By being flexible and open to new opportunities, creators can ensure their content remains engaging and competitive in a constantly evolving media environment.

Embracing Technological Advancements

Technology plays a crucial role in shaping how content is created and consumed. Innovations in artificial intelligence, virtual production, and interactive media are transforming digital entertainment. Staying informed about these advancements helps creators incorporate new tools that enhance production quality and audience experience.

High-quality visuals and sound have become more accessible with cameras, microphones, and editing software improvements. Investing in better equipment over time ensures a professional look and feel, keeping pace with industry standards. Cloud-based production tools allow for remote collaboration, making working with teams from anywhere in the world easier.

Live streaming and real-time audience interaction have also become significant trends, allowing content creators to engage directly with viewers. Shows incorporating interactive elements, such as live Q&A sessions, polls, or virtual reality experiences, provide audiences with a more immersive and engaging format. Experimenting with these technologies keeps content fresh and appealing to a digitally savvy audience.

Adapting to New Platforms

Consumer behavior constantly shifts, and audience preferences change as new platforms gain popularity. A show that thrives on one platform today might need to expand to other spaces to reach its full potential. Diversifying distribution channels ensures that content remains accessible to a wide audience, regardless of where they prefer to watch.

Short-form video platforms like TikTok, Instagram Reels, and YouTube Shorts have changed how audiences consume content. Viewers increasingly prefer bite-sized, engaging clips that capture attention quickly. Repurposing longer content into shorter highlights for these platforms increases discoverability and draws in new viewers who may later engage with full-length episodes.

Podcasting is another avenue for content expansion. Many successful video-based shows repurpose their content into an audio format, allowing audiences to consume episodes while commuting, exercising, or multitasking. Adding transcripts and subtitles to videos also improves accessibility and caters to diverse audiences.

Staying adaptable means recognizing when an emerging platform presents an opportunity. While being active on every platform may not be practical, strategically choosing where to focus efforts based on audience preferences ensures continued growth. Monitoring engagement trends helps determine which platforms are worth prioritizing.

Shifts in Consumer Behavior

Viewer habits evolve, and staying in tune with these changes helps shape content strategies. Audiences today expect authenticity, transparency, and a more personal connection with the creators they follow. Shows that foster community engagement, whether through social media interactions, behind-the-scenes content, or direct viewer participation, strengthen loyalty and long-term retention.

Subscription-based models and membership communities have gained traction as audiences become more willing to support creators directly. Offering exclusive content, early access, or personalized experiences for dedicated fans creates additional value and financial sustainability.

Data-driven decision-making is another key factor in understanding audience preferences. Analyzing viewership patterns, engagement metrics, and feedback provides valuable insights into what works and needs improvement. Regularly reviewing this data ensures content remains aligned with audience interests and adapts to emerging trends.

Maintaining Creativity While Adapting

While embracing new trends and technologies is important, preserving a show's creative essence is equally vital. Chasing trends without a clear strategy can lead to inconsistency and dilute the show's identity. Striking a balance between innovation and authenticity ensures that adaptations feel natural rather than forced.

Experimentation allows creators to test new formats, features, and content styles without overhauling their approach. Small changes, such as integrating new segment types, refreshing visual branding, or exploring different storytelling techniques, keep content fresh without losing the original appeal.

The future of content creation is dynamic, and the ability to evolve is essential for long-term success. Embracing new technologies, expanding to relevant platforms, and staying attuned to shifting viewer expectations all contribute to a sustainable and engaging show. Those who adapt while maintaining creativity and authenticity will continue to grow, ensuring their content remains relevant in an ever-changing media landscape.

Cultivating a Long-Term Vision

Sustaining success in the long run requires more than just talent and effort—it demands a clear vision, ethical responsibility, and a commitment to continuous improvement. In a fast-changing media landscape, staying relevant isn't just about following trends but also about maintaining authenticity, refining skills, and ensuring that content aligns with long-term goals. A show that evolves with purpose maintains integrity, fosters personal and professional growth, and stands a greater chance of lasting impact and continued audience engagement.

Upholding Ethical Standards

A strong foundation of ethics and professionalism is essential for long-term credibility. Audiences value honesty, transparency, and responsible content creation. Ensuring that information is accurate, giving credit where it's due, and respectfully treating guests and audience members contribute to building a trustworthy brand.

Sponsored content, collaborations, and monetization should also be handled with integrity. Disclosing paid partnerships, avoiding misleading advertising, and endorsing only products or services that align with personal values strengthen audience trust. Viewers appreciate creators who prioritize ethical decision-making over short-term financial gains.

Respecting audience diversity is another key factor in maintaining credibility. A broad and varied viewership means different backgrounds, perspectives, and sensitivities must be considered when producing content. Thoughtful communication, inclusive storytelling, and openness to feedback help create a welcoming environment where everyone feels valued.

Investing in Personal Growth

A successful creator is always learning. Expanding knowledge, refining skills, and staying updated on industry advancements contribute to continued improvement. Whether improving storytelling techniques, mastering new editing software, or studying audience behavior, ongoing education helps maintain a competitive edge.

Networking with other professionals, attending workshops, and engaging in industry discussions provide valuable insights and opportunities for growth. Learning from those with more experience, seeking mentorship, or collaborating with diverse voices brings fresh perspectives and prevents creative stagnation.

Personal well-being also plays a role in long-term success. Avoiding burnout, maintaining a healthy work-life balance, and setting realistic goals ensure the creative process is enjoyable rather than exhausting. Sustainable growth happens when content creators prioritize both professional progress and personal well-being.

Consistently Improving Content and Strategy

Evolution is necessary to keep a show engaging over time. While maintaining a recognizable style is important, improving production quality, storytelling, and audience interaction prevents stagnation. Periodic evaluations of what works and what doesn't allow for strategic adjustments that enhance content without compromising authenticity.

Listening to audience feedback, experimenting with new formats, and integrating innovative approaches help refine the show's identity while keeping it dynamic. Small but consistent upgrades—whether through improved visuals, clearer messaging, or more interactive elements—ensure that content remains fresh and engaging.

Long-term success isn't just about numbers; it's about impact. A show continuously adapting while maintaining its ethical foundation and commitment to growth builds a lasting legacy. By embracing change with a clear vision and a dedication to excellence, content creators can sustain relevance and continue to inspire, inform, and entertain for years.